# DREAMER

## Poems in Culture

Alan Botsford

# Also by Alan Botsford

*Possessions: Poems in American Poetry* (2022)
*mamaist: a different sort of light* (2019)
*Walt Whitman of Cosmic Folklore* (2010)
*A Book of Shadows* (2003)
*mamaist: learning a new language* (2002)

For a moment of night, we have a glimpse of ourselves and of
our world islanded in its stream of stars…

–Beryl Markham


I dream in my dream all the dreams of the other dreamers, and I
become the other dreamers.

—Walt Whitman


Eager to rise, now ready for the stars.

—Dante Alighieri

# Author's Note

This book—inspired by and a journey in contemporary culture high and low, east and west in ekphrastic reflections, among others—forms a companion volume with my previous book, *Possessions: Poems in American Poetry*, which explores the lives and works of American poets, from Whitman on. Written mostly between 2010 and 2017, it is an attempt to lay bare the workings of the shadow economy rooted in vernacular energies, exploring how our rational thought process is linked to our dream life. My life in Japan and the Japanese people have made possible the writing of it, for which I remain deeply grateful.

A.B.

Kamakura, Japan

# Contents

# Preludes

# Evening

What's your take, your reading of
the situation, of the moment we live in,
is the crux of this (dark) matter, that
amplitude paves no way ahead through
to hear the mirrored voices, save as powers
yielded to, not contested for, othered
on the sly, from on high, de-selved, or
un-selved, or re-selved as flowers
gamely grown on ground ceded
to, for the fertile heart, unseen, sown.

I know you can't live with this thing,
but we can't take it away from you.

I've heard of many challenges,
but this takes the cake.

Whatever you take me for
is for you to make new, says the world.

For every word we say
making our day,
night is remaking
with imagination's takes.

my take   on what we're    living through   right now
depends   on reading    the cultural moment
as a    palimpsest     of voices

In soundless beats,  as in a trance   we enter
for poetry's dance,   this time     this space

take after take   after take,   then   the final wrap
but not before   every last   scene's   been imprinted
on the heart,   as a living   tattoo   of poetic art.

From our quantum entanglements—including
spooky actions at a distance—is woven
what we call space-time continuum, says
one recent physicist, and who can disagree,
as we go about our business, as we
tangle our way up into this radioed air?

# Mars Aligning

—after an article in *The New York Times,* March 16, 2001


once upon a time, the poem says, this poem was a novel world.
    but ultimately, it goes on, poetry is about connecting
        resources. harnessing the innate power
            of the large network we call language.


imagine activity on a colossal scale that deforms you during
    an early period of your history, but also may spawn
        a warm, wet environment which is necessary
            to foster life, the poem says...


imagine that the ejection of an enormous load of material from
    deep inside you creates the so-called poem—a broad
        elevated region towering above its surroundings.
            the scale of the activity is so huge that it


creates not only a huge trough around the poem, but also
    makes a titanic bulge on the opposite side of it, the so-
        called reader... it also transforms the climate.
            emotions released by the lines of


the poem may create, the poem hints, an atmospheric
    greenhouse sufficient to warm the poem to above freezing,
        allowing running feelings & a flow of ideas to carve
            out the meanings beneath the poem's surface.


according to the mantra of what you need for the life
    of a poem, you need words, energy and images (like organic

compounds). so there are words here, and conditions
are probably above freezing. in so far

as this supports the life of the poem, this is the point. not that a
poem exists here, but suggesting merely that conditions are
favorable. what I'm doing, says the poem, is providing a
connection to how the poem becomes warm and wet.

it's a long stretch to say that that's a condition (for a poem),
that's for sure. that, the poem says, is not to be implied.
it does imply, however, that inspiration is available
for the life of the poem if other factors are favorable...

imagine that the poem is a beach ball and that your 'reading' of
it is your fist. as your fist pushes into the beach ball, there
is a bulge created on the opposite side of the ball, a
depression or trough that surrounds your fist.

it's that simple.

this event (of 'reading') explains the irregular shape
and the gravity field of the rest of your world. (the scale of
poetic output or inspiration from any given poem is
unique as far as we know it in the Solar System.)

readers have noticed that the network of meanings in a poem
may resemble Earth's river systems. other readers say many
of the poem's meaning systems must have formed after a
significant amount of the poetic load was in place.

the meanings may reflect the clement conditions caused by
large amounts of combustion and decomposition of words,
as organic substances, resulting from the poem's use of
language. at the end of the poem, poetic activity

dissipates and your emotions and ideas are removed from the
atmosphere by a combination of factors—including
stripping by the solar wind and thermal escape, among
others. the removal of emotions and ideas would drive

the poem's surface temperature below freezing. this process,
the poem says, could unfold in a split second, or in the time
it takes a human being to be born, live and die, depending
upon the poem, and who the readers of it are, or will be.

let's call the life that precedes this plunge back into cold
a "brief, shining moment" for the poem. yes, the one
you're now reading. so far away yet so close.

# News Headlines from *The End Times*

i

Tranquil Realist Takes Ideal Path to Bargain Basement
of Heaven ("So Far Away Yet So Close") and With Flying Start
Shows the Goods of the Not-So-Good-Old Days,
Stirring Mixed Feelings
"Change is inevitable. But change what?" says one angel.
"Is mystery dying out?" asks another.
"Are you becoming a brand?" says still another.

Wary about Future Adding to the Sufferings of the Past,
Realist Focuses on Immediate Legwork:
"I am part historian, part journalist, part specialist investor…"
"Tilting at windmills?" a chorus of angels asks.
Realist Says 'No' and Cometh to a Conclusion:
"I see nothing but darkness ahead of me."
"This, in being said, is a ray of sun!" an angel shouts.

ii  take

Top billing in titles these days?
Frost, Oldenburg, Issa, the Sabine Women.
So much praising, anyone's in the public market—
Simone Weil, Dante Alighieri, Borges, Breughel,
Bucephalus, even the body of a dog.
Chardin's wife, too, joins the chronicle of
curtain calls and close calls.
While here, constantly so near and
confessing a certain something, is
Petrarch, the Devil, Ed.

Why, even Love at the entrance to the Underworld
puts on a new face in this exchange.
The fathers are all here, fear not.
The figures even Sappho forgave.
The good mother, grace, saying goodbye
to the old life, gone to the devil...
A grateful man's house visited by
gravity, grief, and growth
with gusto, growing at the speed
of fashion and the ways in which
we matter, like these heavenly bodies:
Roy Orbison, Harpo, Horace.
House with its own island,
with *homo erectus* home to roost
in an improbable story, until
Ovid intrudes... and Kepler... King Lear.
It takes all kinds just to say it:
Leonardo's bicycle in a land bountiful,
a library of skulls, little epics of oblivion.
Lost in translation, like Lot's wife...
magical thinking makes Maria Callas appear on Broadway
—matriarch of the meadows of memory—
while not even men throwing bricks
will stop Ashbery's milk train.
The names of history, my father explains,
are necessary and impossible swans (not all, only a few return).
Now's not the end of the world ordinarily
but offering, like luminous ordinariness, one hundred
versions of the peaceable kingdom, one self at a time,
is the only way: Garcia Lorca, Hart Crane, Ophelia over the
pond, (the owl our nature). Paul Klee passes by.
Pause, pause... Edward James (printer's error?),
Chopin, Psyche, Plato, Richard Nixon.

The river rising and falling, rising
past dawn where Robert Bly's ruthless radiance
will not testify. Shhh... Samuel Johnson's saying things,
but the scientists explain: sea washes sand scours sea between
waves. Sentimental self-reflections of shadow,
hawk, and dove—sightseers, like Sisyphus, turning
up for the show and tell, for the sudden lightness.
Take my neighbor—the model to which I've held.
Take toddlers and parents. Take Alice to the moon.
Take umbrage under the cloud, under water, behind glass,
at these unquiet ones, these vanishing points...
No victory but a wake-up call (Was it Stella, or Was it Stella?).
Washing my face in the wave: What can be said, whatever it is,
is what happens, is what you will remember:
the white lie, the wide-eyed look, the wish that won't let go.
The world, the wreckage, and the wrap.


iii


2$^{nd}$ time Around, Realist Slipping Through a Crack in Time
Gets a Rare Very Fleeting Take-2 at the Top Where
Much Remains to Be Said


"It's official," Realist hears. "To win the judgement of history
Go way back to the graveyard to where side by side in life
(And now in death) the hype goes on... But as for digging out
the truth ..."


"Not so fast!" Realist says. "I'm no big shot!
Besides, there's no easy exit from here!"
And Suddenly Detour Takes Realist to Where
Delicate Mission is Detected:
        Let's come apart at the seams

gently, and return to where the
names come up saying,
 'What have we done to you?'


He Fishes Deep in the Slipstreams of His Mind
And O What a Catch He's Able to Find!
(Every Living Thing Is the Style of Its Content.)
Yes, While History Puts Its Graveyard on the Map, a Savior
(Of Appearances) (Last of a Dying Breed?…Oh C'mon!)
Hauls Up From These Depths the Catch of the Day and
Quickly…Reverently… Throws It Back.


*


Trawling lines hauled in for the catch arrayed in sound
and rhythm is the poem writing itself, Fisherman.

# Apocalypse Coming Soon Enough

i

Storming the gates of paradise
by way of the 'gateless gate'
will, I've learned, get you nowhere fast.
Sooner slow down
the tempo, and cultivate
serenity
in the face of hate,
than win any prizes from
The State,
who begs—like hell they do—
to differ on every account
save one: your payment
is never too late.


ii

Guilty of beginner's mind
again—I'm the one guarding
all those babies—is not the same
thing as seeing angels in the trees
—I'm always too late,
too conscious of the
tree being cut down—
or tiger in the skies—Mr. Blake
beat me to the punch—but
whatever the hell I'm seeing now
I can't tell the end of. After all we're
adults, we work till kingdom come.

You've been talking in your sleep again.

We go out into the world to make
the world in us out of words
both lasting and passing—
our private mythologies, public realities—
epiphanies being belatedly felt
in the body's growing ache.

It's a shame I'm not a book
It's a shame I'm not a book
O the things you could learn
if I were a book
You'd need only open me.

iii

Metonymy, not metaphor
I'll work for,
is his creed,
no artsy screed
but licing a host
for a ghosty ride
into hell and
back again, with the tide,
though he won't swift boat
metaphor either. Rather,
he'll Ferdinand it under
the tree of life and
sigh over some clover…
No clarion call to a war
that can never be won
until wholeness is one

with self at its elemental
best, core of the mind
embodying what matters
most to creation's imagination
(before form is eaten away):
That nature has some bowels,
and the poet some balls.


Everything, everything that we know of
as 'the world' depends on love
to keep it turning, turning
into something other
than what it was,
the poet thinks, as
he wonders—
Is it me that's
broken, or the celestial machinery?
And who, or what,
can fix it?


iv


The best a parasite can hope to do
is become a host for the host,
which in a way he was doing
whenever he lets himself channel
the voices he hears coming in
over the radio waves of the times,
he a radio station in their midst
playing 'host' to their thoughts
and writing them down
in that brief space where there's
neither host nor guest.

v


He instigates a revolution
in the thought processes
of his readers.
An intrepid moralist, he
sees into the heart—
Black or white or red or
yellow or brown—
and says, Love
moves mountains, traverses valleys
and fords rivers
in the name of all
Creation.
How beautiful.
It doesn't mean it's true,
unless you
are beautiful too.


vi


The world's meaningfulness
and the world's randomness
meet at night.
Its code is what humans
must learn to decipher
if we are to make the
next move, the next step
forward as a species.
The science of dreams is
the science of the future.

We live in images
because we dream them.
They are our original language.

This is your
stint in the underworld
of your pain.
Time for to let it rain.
Though one can't remove the human stain,
stay sane
and faithful
to your dreams.

vii

Our body is our life
as the original wife.
Guard her purity
against needless strife,
or pay the price of war.
The spiritual journey's
for the whore
called to know her worth
every step of the fallen way.
(The booty stolen
is the body fallen.)

*Ai*, point energy. It's what
love is and does.

A keeper's way forward:
love is, and does,
a kind of rocksteady grace

in the face of the mind
that matters and the body, in tatters,
sailing an ocean of stars
where it senses
nothing is lost
that is loosed
into what lasts.

For the body, it
does the thinking,
does the feeling,
does the moving,
does the imagining,
does the understanding,
in good times or bad,
does the changing—
chrysalis to imago—
that space creates
over time.

viii

Anna Karenina – She was crushed
under the wheels
of history. Or, Tolstoy's imagination.

Nation means history.

How do you find the proper
balance between honoring
the past and obsessing over it?

To live and breathe apocalypse
without any need to write about it,
is to live in Japan where
last things are first and where
first things… last.


The heart jewels are
the real stars


But the imploding star generates
some heat.


Our intimate cameraman of the now
hears the planet and apes it
till his kingdom come,
as a wet-nurse to the psyche.
He mouths no platitudes
save one: Homeboy of hell,
save me the next match,
for I am one with thee,
continuity evolved in history.


Lion lying in the sand,
the waves of the past
washing over him.


The dream I'm trying to wake up from,
says the poet, is one that says I won't survive
its telling, the way the butterfly emerges from
its chrysalis to be born, unfolding its wings to fly.

# Dream Project

The poetry machine that'll chew me up
and spit me out, I write in fear of.

Trust your deep, energetic years.

Tell your story so others will know hell
does not last forever.

Every night I write a poem in my sleep: it's called dreaming.

Dreams are my original poems
read through the night,
now color, now black and white,
imagining trope-less sight
experiencing its own power,
as words arrive downstream later.

Dreams never lie; reality definitely does.

Dreams are catalysts—
they convert nighttime
energy into daytime truths.

The names I have ghosted come back
to haunt me in the house of my lack—
out of their echoes this room I make
in the rounding journey I have yet to take
now leaving right in love's wake.

Revive ancient practices
for future use & understanding

What's been lost to the modern soul costs us dear.
But in searching, one may find it lying buried
in one's dreams, a language spoken in the night
that resonates all day long through one's flesh
and in one's very bones and that takes shape as
myriad (unconscious) thoughts in the (night) mind.

He loves the ways the subconscious works,
not without reason, not without rhyme,
that succors the spirit such as no other
human discourse can. It announces:
the unseen has its voice, the unheard
has its body, and where the twain meet
conspires the soul which the conscious
mind would, by modern accounts, dismiss.

We make our own movies. – but "It's only a movie," said Alfred
Hitchcock.
We make our own dreams. — but "It's only a dream," we all
say.

says the dreamer—
I hereby take ownership of my sleep,
and assimilate the dreams herein where
good or bad whatever is said or done
reverberates in my waking life whether
or not I know it or bow to it or wait for it
to reveal its secrets to me incessantly.
My sleep in whose images I invest
with meaning with significance with love
that it will repay me in kind night and day
My sleep in whose knowledge I believe
whether or not I grasp what it's saying
My sleep whose trifles I assimilate

into my consciousness for larger stakes
to come, my sleep, my sleep my soul to keep.

What if the phantasmorgia of everyday life
were observable with detachment,
like a scientist conducting an experiment?

Dreaming, as the Aborigines understood, is the art of the human.
For them, waking every morning from a night of dreaming
must have been like a EUREKA experience.

The past and future both dream
in the present, of change. Sleep's images
de-tox the body at night and are re-arranged in
the day's charges, positive or negative.
Time won't stay whole any other way.

A new science of poetry and dreams
is what he's angling for, mark his deeds…

No, it's the language of dreams, language
as dream.

Everyone has an epic narrative within.
Cosmic currents of everyday odysseys—

Accurate demonstrations, en masse, of the hidden creative springs
and workings in sleep, of the dreaming mind, are what is needed.

Alan lies
in a bed of his own making,
but what a bed it is!
The dreams he sees and hears
are star-like in their appearance,
Earth-bound in their destination,

and sun-stolen in their reach.
But what is he guilty of
exactly, but of imagining
a way forward we can all follow,
were our imaginations big enough,
our spirits wide enough,
our loves deep enough
to say what needs saying
in our own day, our own way, shy of
his prayer we would all do well
to hear. Amen.

It's a spiritual way
you've founded, and a potential breakthrough
in everything from psychology, to dreams,
to illness, to language, to pilgrimage, and to
traditions scientific, literary & religious.
The ramifications are both breath-
taking and far-reaching.

Dreams as process, and more. Dreams as dialogue, as learning,
as source of a faith grounded in scientific or empirical study.
It should go a long way in restoring a lost balance. We each
have the means at our disposal, he keeps telling us.
He's awe-inspiring.…The rest is off the table for now!

…the uses of Gandhian non-violence for self-liberation
…retrieving ancient lore for modernity?

It would be one of the great
projects of our time,
if luck will hear you.

I'd do it if I were you.
I'd do it in a flash.

# Nighttime

i  (in)takes


While we're worshipping in the church
of Time is Money,


the moon yearns to be
back up in the sky.


*


An owl has a face
you don't see
at night, its hooting
suffices for what passes as 'owl,'
as the nocturnal music
seeps into your consciousness
via what's hidden in the dark.


*


Wired to a nighttime sky brimming with stars,
how many of us experience the visitation of 'the gods' or spirits
by way of celebrities appearing in our dreams? A commonplace,
I'm certain.

In a dream one night I heard a voice say to me:
Talking to God? angels? tutelary spirits? disincorporated souls?
Welcome, poet, to the annals of manic disquiet… Which raises
the question, to whom does your language belong? asks
the man with butterfly antennae

…which later made me think about my dreamlife these past dark years during which I've taught poetry to Naomi Osaka; watched Jessica Alba being arrested in front of my childhood home; seen Gary Cooper with long, hippy hair; talked with Kirk Douglas; warned Roger Federer of a fire; been a middle-aged man named 'Daniel Craig;' had Marilyn Monroe ask me about my privates; seen fifty kids throw baseballs all at once toward Shohei Ohtani as he stood in the outfield, forcing him to choose which one he'll catch; brought my new poetry book to show Shuntaro Tanikawa at his traditional house, only to discover after opening the box that it was *his* book; had poet William Heyen advise, 'It's good to have talent, but don't tell the neighbors'; watched Novak Djokovic somersault over a fence and leap hundreds of feet below, landing uninjured; celebrated the motorcycle-riding skills of Steve McQueen; had Paul McCartney sprinkle gold glitter over my head; had Adam Driver walk out on me in the middle of a conversation; met Yusef Komunyakaa at a beach house he called the 'preview house'; conversed with Toni Morrison outdoors in a garden while she was gardening; met Joni Mitchell in a garage as she coolly gave me a raised middle finger; attended a conference on the Goddess Aphrodite with the late poet-critic Morgan Gibson; had Maya Angelou incorrectly issue me a stomach cancer diagnosis which I flatly rejected; visited Joseph Brodsky's home where he was hosting a Christmas party; heard Alice Walker encourage a young Black poet doubting himself; made it one night with Simona Halep, and on another night with Sarah Connor; met and befriended elderly Ian McKellan and Patrick Stewart; taken Japanese lessons from Peter Barakan; discussed films with Bradley Cooper; drunk beer with the actor 'The Rock'; met the new James Bond who, while holding a pistol, said, 'I am nothing if I can't flick my dick'; had Christopher Plummer show me an esoteric book by W.B. Yeats; played tennis on a clay court with Walt Whitman; seen

J.D. Salinger deliver three new stories in a large envelope to his publisher's office with a note attached saying: 'Put it in their lives,' and then seen his editor, a stately woman, and his publisher, a tall man, come out into the hallway and embrace him warmly in a group hug, crying tears of joy; and taken a class with Barack Obama where we discussed being 'broken' and how the time of Emerson's 'powering over the gaps' is over…

…Double-take the giver's dream
nothing is what his river seems.


Nights are hard to get through
but days end too soon.
I watch dreams bleed
through the filters of fog before they lift
into language I have no words for.
Time to settle the accounts
foisted on me by history
I hardly know. But
the questions keep coming
as headlines that bait us
to read on and on.


ii  double takes


why the sudden jolt of energy when laying eyes upon a celeb?
call it 'spine-tingling,' if you will.


when?  years ago…  where?   New York City…
where stars and celebs     sauntered down sidewalks
in full public view,    though we mustn't say so…
sshhh   let them pass, sans salutation   save in the mind's eye
now (there's nowhere else I need to be)

…there's huge Orson Welles in a thick overcoat and a bright red scarf slowly driving by in a golf cart alongside Radio City Music Hall… there's black-clad Salvador Dali and Gala sitting together at a table solemnly eating lunch in the Russian Tea Room… there's lanky Donald Sutherland with his petite French wife momentarily locking eyes with me and my date one evening in an Upper West Side parking garage… there's Robin Williams as he walks out of Forbidden Planet comics store in the East Village staring curiously at my wife, infant son and me before he vanishes into the summer crowds… there's middle-aged, debonair James Mason one spring evening in a long overcoat strolling down Park Avenue… there's white-haired Andy Warhol, surrounded by his entourage, strolling across St. Mark's Square on a Saturday night… there's rake-thin Jerzy Kozinski, jaw jutting out, briskly walking along 57th Street on a hot July afternoon… there's willowy, Tolkien-charactered Seamus Heaney standing beside me at the urinal in the men's room of the Guggenheim Museum… there's imposing Sandra Bernhard all in black striding up to an East Village deli counter, laughingly barking her order to the clerk… there's low-key Philip Glass, dressed in black, buying bagels at a 2nd Avenue deli... there's Isabella Rossellini in a tweed overcoat and scarf strolling past near Washington Square… there's Woody Allen with a female companion gliding by on the Upper East Side near Central Park…

…And later, slick, streamlined Alfa Romeo-like Italo Calvino…
and imperious owl, courtly, unruffled Czeslaw Milosz…
and ghostly shaman, otherworldly Sphinx Jorge Luis Borges…
and intellectual doyenne meets Hollywood starlet Jorie Graham…
and feline, leonine Elizabeth Hardwick…
and prissy, bitchy, preening Richard Howard…
and quizzical, aloof, artful Mark Strand…

and proud, delicate Derek Walcott...
and with blond wife by his side, dark-skinned, clear-eyed Octavio Paz...
and warm, cuddly wild scholar with bite & growl Stanley Kunitz...
and fame's darling, a walking icon on the prowl for lovers Allen
Ginsberg...
and thunderstruck, jokey prophetess Annie Dillard...
and force of language, no fool-brooker Joseph Brodsky...
and poetic, hard-jawed asethete Stephen Sandy...
and bourgeois necro-sciencer Madeline L'Engle...
and roly-poly mystic, pro-wrestler of Buddhism the Dalai Lama...

Mars aligning, Venus rising,
navigating by the stars...

The believers will keep
coming to turn the
tide, if he doesn't
hide what it's been like
being him all these years.

There's something about human
beings being able to dream.

What's the story? Animals
everywhere dream.

He clears a path direct
into dream thought,
unfiltered, uncensored,
unbelievable!

Surrealists were doing that
a long time ago.

Not like this, they weren't.
There's a moral center here,
not random or arbitrary,
almost cosmic. I kid you not.
And while preserving nature, he serves culture.

He hasn't convinced me yet.
Meanwhile, I'll drag his name
through mud…

So this is what poetry does, I thought,
tuning in while turning out –

And there, out among the stars, the silences streaming inward
to tell of joys the darkness, unstinting, gives and gives,
is the light of the moon unseen by the poet dreaming:

The ghost of now
that occasionally
visits here.

I'm here with you.
I witness.
I listen.

We tear away
the wrappings
and lay our
ear to the ground.

# The American

i    early

The American lives by his wits
if the future has any say in the matter
He lives or dies by no code other
than his pursuit of say opposites
tragic comic happy sad slave master
The whole rigamarole stacked against
him and still his fears dispensed
with tomorrow being another day
and life being no morality play
save for the ingenuity bits.
Whatever it takes to get
the job done, the imaginative world
—the competition be damned—
fully alive and invested in,
where his moment of truth
is every moment of earth
and heaven, silent as death.
This is how creation works,
what his mind alone makes
possible on its way
into the news that stays news,
a bio that reads like the day
he gave his soul to his muse(s)
and never looked back.

ii  late

He has balls
that are galling
to the walls
that only close in
on themselves. He
of no false heart
keeps giving his takes
and taking the hits,
for he knows better
than to call
this hall of mirrors
real.

He'd peel back veils
and peer into hells
he knows nothing of,
believing love
will save
what needs saving.
But loss won't have
any of his folly.
Loss punctures the
balloon he rides in,
the bubble he walks
inside of: gone, gone…
always clear
about images tossed
into a heap
over which he'd
learn, finally, to weep.

# Part One

*He commanded the stars*
*to shine in heaven,*
*and they did.*

# John Berger

British art critic     i.m. 2017

i  (his voice)  —after *Ways of Seeing*

I can say my way of seeing depends on how
I say what I see, and for this, we unlearn
as much as we learn, to see again what is.
Time can stop. Space can collapse. We are
subject to differing dimensions by virtue
of how we do our seeing, the ways in which
we say what we see. The film is one way.
The photograph is another. The advertisement
is still another. Context is everything. We imbue
the object of our gaze with meanings by the apparatus
that frames it. Nothing is settled, except for
the stillness and the silence of the image
itself, which, whether genuine or replicated,
is transmittable, even across space and time,
and returns us, to our surprise, to our naked eye.

ii  Susan Sontag, American writer, in conversation with
    John Berger, YouTube video 1983   (her voice)

I see behind your eyes a deep-souled man,
one for whom words are passages to other
places and times that work our imaginations
in a humanizing direction. Your voice gives
a sense and range of your humanity that I find
marvelous, but also thrilling, since into those

depths I'm privileged to enter with you and freely
roam. It's an adventure let's call intellectual.
Love may have little to do with it, yet has
everything to do with it, too. Thanks to your
vision I find new things to say, a journey
I don't wish to end any time soon. Male
perception clarified by life in the French rural
countryside, by choice—an astonishing one,
too, in this day and age. False brilliance you
won't indulge speaks well of you, the patched
together framework of our talk notwithstanding.
I have my eye on the telling detail, which makes
for a good fit, properly speaking mind you. We
won't stray off course where I go. Besides, it's
too public and risky a venue to do that. More
private concerns must take a backseat to the
public stand we make here together, on the art
of storytelling, in a crisis of sorts, with the
narratives no longer controlled, now up for grabs.
Where does it lead us, and who will read us?
Attitudes and opinions I have in abundance,
while yours is a complementary sense
of the poetic and the sublime.

iii  Scott Esposito, American writer, on John Berger
     and George Orwell, 2017  (his voice)


The men who wrote the books that spoke
to me had fought in a war that was lost
but not, today, lost to us as justice spreads
from its pages in ways I can only praise
and marvel at, and share with others its
wonders that still speak to me and inspire

me despite the fires in the world gone out.
We have an obligation to read those books
and talk about them, that their justice
can be passed along and belong to us
again in the present. We hear that song
of the novelist or critic who staked his life
in a sense of justice his writing can prolong,
and we give thanks, and note the price paid,
and carry its torch forward into the fray.


iv  Annie Julia Wyman, American writer, on
      John Berger, 2017  (her voice)


Anything I can say about the man John Berger
cannot come close to the art that he made
of his thoughts, his mode of perception being
'the story' as it is told from the ancient stock
of humanity, the stone turned upright being
the marker of before and after that his life,
now in death, has come to stand for. The poet
of death, then, in love with life, with pleasure
at the core of being, which he saw through
and wrote about and embodied. A Meister
given social status by virtue of a critical
thought process divining otherness as
the truth of our existence, that anything less
is a sham, an hierarchical ploy, an historical
retreat into the self-cannibalizing human being.
This death-haunting gives life its meaning,
yes, but more than that, it gives art its structure,
its underpinning, roots and all, which flowers
into consciousness as the root wonder of any
existence we call sentient. That his spoke

from the depths without inflating the
historical ego speaks volumes of his sense
of compassion and justice, his human touch.


v    John Berger  (his voice)


Given what we know, the truth-
telling instinct and the story-
telling instinct only randomly
overlap, it being the work of
human reason to invent the
narratives that get us closer
to what passes for the truth
which, objectively speaking,
is subject to change, given
its connection to the flux
which we understand so little of.


vi  Ben Lerner, American writer, on
     John Berger, 2017  (his voice)


He, John Berger, quietly illumined
the sun setting on capitalism, and
brought understanding to the fogs
of discourse that reveals a timeless
grasp of things concrete and ephemeral
both, a poet's sensibility at play in
the fields of the world, the past
his proper palette as only a painter
could brush in the layers thick with
meaning, of our relations to it and
to one another. He infused his prose,
too, with magnetic insights that stick

with you, ways of seeing things that
brush aside the wallpaper for the surfaces
beneath. He brought depth to everything
he saw, and described what he saw
in effortless prose. I will miss the authority
of the man, and the humanity of the author.

*

We startle the cosmos of language
into becoming alternate universes
where we can breathe in and live
other lives, for a start. Novels or
poems can do this, but only as
an engine of imagination which
reality, strangely enough, needs.

# John Kaag

American philosopher

(his voice)  —after *American Philosophy*

i

To have borne witness to the starry words
of thinkers past, through the lonely night
on the hilltop to the dawning light of
morning, is to have cleared a small path
to the present moment where, just maybe,
my words will carry some of their weight
and, like stardust, bless us with their memory.

ii  trespassing night

Words being dangerously said are
dangerous words, no matter the star
uttered beneath, save one: Let down
the bars, O Death, hear what I say.

# Saul Williams

American singer-songwriter

(his voice) —after an interview, 2015

Go and
make things
Enjoy things.

Tidy up…

On the verge of
the global city.

Let's say it in the interval, baby.

The city & the showman
put up a fight.

Inner amputee
of the war.

Calyxes of pride & flattering.

I dance, it wasn't
step nigga.

Forgotten fabulist
on a roll.

*Jowl* & *Sheaves*
*of Grass* are
my favorite books.

Let me talk
a book free for us,
it'll be titled
'Free for Us'

The earthquake registers
high voltage in the area
of the mind.

The rotting city
and Coriolanus make
good bedmates.

I've earned the right
to please where I please.

Hollow muse anchored
in the law.

Now toast is rotten,
the feast paid for
by the ill-gotten.

Hammer it hard how
hardness holds up.

Disasters delight the mind
in its ham-fisted way.

Hours ago time
spent itself.

To be a disturbing person
has been a lifelong dream,
we seem stuck in the suburbs
of the imagination.

# Pharoah Sanders

American jazz saxophonist  i.m.


i  (his voice)    —after the *New Yorker* interview, 2020


Time played to
gives me space
to find out
what I'm thinking
or feeling, but
no note ever feels
right unless
the reed fits
the mouthpiece,
which is rare.
I got to explore
sound that others
don't think of
as beautiful, and
try to make it
sound beautiful.
That for me
is worth the trip.


ii  —after "The Creator Has a Master Plan"


'spiritual jazz' plunks you down
in the middle of your humanity
where the soul has a place its own
and where spirit travels freely,

telling a story you long to hear
being told, lost in the tear
that falls as you listen,
your karma now in transition
to your body's newest edition,
this via music your religion
that all art aspires to the condition of
—though, face it, where's the love?

# Joan Baez

American folksinger

Bleeding heart panders to the bone
in us all. How far does that get her,
she's asked in so many words, the
hardness surrounding her now by
which institutions stand and fall.
She replies from the high road, many
missing her point, some not, as she
unknots the closed fist and reaches
out, not to hold hands but to listen,
just listen to what others have to say.
The low roaders either way
will walk away.

# Martin Luther King Jr.

—after *Selma*, dir. Ava DuVernay

Martin Luther King Jr moved it around:
He flowed in as a pastor, grew into an activist,
blossomed as a civil rights leader, and
was martyred at only 39. His story tells
of glory won from the high road taken
when the low road rose to greet him,
armed and dangerous.

# Marshall McCluhan

Canadian philosopher

Wedded to the here
and now, the culture critic waxes
and wanes, the burned off fog
of obfuscation revealing a
pandering to literary fame and
fortune culled from corporate
bastions he formerly had joy
in taking down.

# Chelsea Manning (b. Bradley Manning)

American Army whistleblower, ex-Federal prisoner, activist

(her voice)

Hon, we won the day
but lost the night and
now tarrying in darkness,
I carry the stigma of
my love for you, you who
aroused my sense of outrage
and injustice into deed I
cannot regret yet am convicted by.

# Cristóvão Ferreira

17th century Portuguese Jesuit priest

—after *Silence,* dir. Martin Scorsese

The fallen priest clenches his teeth
in the jaws of despair, and flinches.
No guilt is this white man's burden
taken to the heart of Asian darkness
where his followers, in hot pursuit,
seek the glory of their god. They meet
their original nature and become lost
to god, who does not answer, it seems,
their prayers. The cicadas sing,
however, as the Christians suffer their
trial of faith, the Buddhists having found
what they offer, wanting. Though
the power of hearing one's own inner voice
cannot, as Endo Shusaku reminds us,
be underestimated for its beauty and grace.

# Toni Morrison

American novelist


i   (her voice) 2017


Whites have struck a bargain with the Devil
and it is with themselves. Hard the way
has been, of 'sacrifice' at the altar of color.
We have seen what it has wrought, death
being cheap for people of color, and civil
war is not far behind. Pray tell, who do we
think we are in America, but whiteness
privileged beyond the decencies, on display
in the red white and blue we can no longer
be true to. The source of our righteous
anger has been deeply tapped in the wake
of this election, and the man now in the seat
of power will wreak havoc with our lives
beyond what words dare say. We cherish
the outgoing president as one of us, he
of biracial birth, who showed us today
what tomorrows can be made of. His wife
will take us there, we hope, some other day.


*


Time allots us stories we can tell
but there's hell to pay along the way,
especially for Black writers. We'd like
to think we're the same as just plain

writers but, in truth, we're not. Our
tales must be told the way we've
lived them—from the margins, from
the darkness of our shared past.
Voices that arise in me tell it their
way, and I just follow, climbing up
out of ignorance and blindness and
into knowledge and light, if possible.
That's when the stakes get high, that's
when the clouds part and the sun shines
down on us all, writer and reader alike.

ii Roxanne Gay, American writer, on
      Toni Morrison  (her voice)


The talent she displayed made mincemeat
of the patriarchy. And I mean she dispensed
with it and elevated the female where
she could dispense her beauty and wisdom.
For this I am forever grateful to her.

# Samantha Hunt

American novelist

(her voice)

I do the patchworking I'm partial to
in part because the whole appears
just as elusive as it's always been,
and who has the time to pursue it?
Let me revel in the bits and pieces
that keep me company in my hours
of reading bliss, that soak through
my skin and course through my
veins, those convincing fragments
that I've shored up against my ruins,
that fit me and my madness to a T.
Everything decays anyway, shored up or not.
It's the repetition of the action itself
that somehow saves the day, the wanting
the same effort to be put into play
again and again regardless of the result,
which is always the same—more ruin.
Keep shoring up those fragments, we say,
against all the odds, and sinisterly the gods
having a lark with us will make it all work.

# Clint Eastwood

American actor, filmmaker

—after *American Sniper*

Let's jazz up the violence
and earn aesthetic marks for
plucking out our enemies' eyes
on screen, so to speak, to the
tune of righteous aggression and
a dollop of complication. Let's
wrap the final battle in a literal and
figurative fog to lend the proceedings
a veneer of moral complexity so
viewers momentarily suffer pangs
of doubt. But let not the show be
stopped (by guilt) but roll on
tooting our horn of democracy
drunk with power projected darkly
and with deadly aim.

# Leonardo DiCaprio & Brad Pitt

American actors

i  Leonardo DiCaprio
  — after *The Revenant*, dir. by Alejandro G. Iñárritu.

Times tarries for no one, not least
for wounded ones in the snow, he
a seeker of revenge. His boy's loss
keeps him alive somehow, to get back
in the end what can never return.
The bear—a witty symbol—bears
the weight of Nature, as the hero's nature
is rent in two, barely kept alive, icy
winter loins making a man out of
the dead horse's innards he eats
before sheltering there inside the animal from
the cold. Nothing's left to our
imagination save the dream he keeps
having, as the ending becomes a dream.

ii  Brad Pitt
  —after *Once Upon a Time in… Hollywood*,
    dir. Quentin Tarantino

He gets to be a badass, kicking
(among others) the iconic Bruce Lee's butt
(who would've kicked Pitt's butt in every
other universe but Tarantino's). Meanwhile,
DiCaprio shows off his acting chops,

from 'bad-acting' to 'good-acting' to 'great-acting,'
even shilling for death-sticks in the credit roll.
The climax is a signature bloodbath of Satan-worshippers
who, bent on killing, get killed off first when Pitt's dog
(a pit-bull of course) gets to do her share of mauling,
the goal being the mauling, or re-writing, of history,
with brutal violence as the means of doing so
('regeneration through violence' by any other name). Why does
one leave, then, the cinema feeling the fictionalizing
of history settles real scores on the people in it and then some?
Fantasy, no worse for wear, obliges. Even puts history on notice.

# Bong Joon Ho

—South Korean filmmaker (his voice)

How do films get made but through
the imagination of the characters
who drive the scenes and the themes
according to the mystery of their
natures. What social critique or
commentary that follows is
circumstantial at best.

You know what it is
the john is dead of.

Touching on the formal properties
of poetry, you discover there is room
for surprise, the shock of recognition
that only language can provide.

*

Or to put it differently—
I have come through fire
to tell you this story,
the flames coalescing into
these words I'm writing.

Get your heart out
of your mouth, I tell
myself. But it stays
there, and it tastes
like hell.

# John le Carré

British spy novelist

(his voice)

I won't whitewash my character
flaws but will distill them through
the characters I create for my books,
which writing tides me over the painful
unpleasantries of life to observe
the secrets of our existence at a remove,
guarded but not cynical, a believer
despite myself, triggering my imagination
to heights and depths of story, thrillingly
always story, plotted by possibility
in the interest of the social contract:
Who are we given our social roles,
and who will we become given
our worst and best impulses, vast
in their permutations, and as mythic?
The humanitarian cause I'd subscribe to
brings redress for all our covert crimes;
the world's overt survival depends on it,
or at least my moral ambiguity's high art does.

# Part Two

*What keeps you down here*
*but the stars you look up at*
*at night?*

# The Comedian

i

Their laughter peals, bell-like, in your ears
announcing *We're yours*, your words
striking to the chord that connects
them to the view that opens and spills
its cry that you would collect like gold coins.
They who are caught in your throes captive
of your body blows reigning down,
your victims now in the touched-on river that
runs through fear and nothingness. And when,
like a ladybug perched on a finger ready to fly,
their rapture ends, you, with no choice in the matter,
let go… your 'power' short-lived, while they—
having laughed heartily, healthily, happily— live long.

ii

Blessed laughter is like a motorcycle
you're riding, engines blazing.
Stay on and don't get off, let the power
take you zooming where it would.
The others—and there are many—
who would warn you, judge you,
act out on you, they'll thicken you with
courage for all their winnowing words.
Be of good cheer and good spirits, letting
the laughter god and his horsepower
wheel you around town, your foot
on the accelerator of space and time.

iii

Play is its own refund
to be used again and again

The oldest joke?
A pundit punned it.

iv

The laughingstock I invest in
restores true value to my life,
the taste of money turned honey.

# Mark Twain

American author, humorist

White, as you know,
is English's favorite color.

English, strong and resilient,
invites other languages to its shores.

While Huck Finn, drifting or
navigating the rapids, loves
Black culture.

The grass he sits on in the noonday sun
leaves poems in its wake.

Democracy fought for
is the war worth fighting.

And youthful English is there
in the trenches or manning
the front lines, hungry for action.

Its rowdy manners belie a delicacy
of feeling that is the envy of other
languages, or so it likes to believe.

With troops amassed
at almost every border,
worldwide acceptance and use

is its real claim to legitimacy,
as the Babel of our times.

Link to everything—

this is a gift
of the English language.

# Charles Chaplin

British comic, filmmaker

'Charlie,' the rose of a thornless flower,
was a thorn in the side of tyranny
everywhere, reveling in his power
of the underdog to undermine cruelty
with heroic dignity for us all,
by remaining ever small.
The part he would not outgrow
became for the whole world a show
beyond vaudeville's limelight,
every day a scene from night
played backwards, the anarchist's right.
What strange metamorphosis he'd undergo
for his Charlieness, high and low,
cannot explain the sublime weight
of a funny man transcending hate,
the clown's awkward grace, the fate
of his antics to suddenly mutate
into the pathos of a humane tableaux:
the penniless tramp not stealing the show
for real-time wealth, just so,
but the kid, say, rising to be a king
of New York, via the theater's darkening
projections in which his bright star
is born, shining on wherever we are.

# Marilyn Monroe

American actress

(her voice)

I have it on good authority my body
speaks every language but one: age.
The double-speak my soul dabbles in dares
men to come to me on my own terms—
young, smart and pretty. I've won the right
from a persona you'll not hear vent,
for happiness is sent only in a present
which is, like me, unwrapped slowly
and with all consideration due a beauty
my time has seen to shape. It's my calling
card, if you will, so everyone knows what
I fight for. Close up, I vacillate between
endings and beginnings in love affairs,
which are nothing if not long shots where
my heart's concerned. The men I've mated
make a woman wish she were all, but
I'm after bigger fish. No, not the femme
fatale but the femme natale, she born
tomorrow out of today's ashes. It's how
I double the trouble I cause. My star,
seemingly high in the sky, hangs low
after all, a low-lying fruit you'd think
is within reach. I haven't the heart to tell
the closer you get, the farther apart we are,

a free-show, I call it, only the lonely know…
Sometimes I wonder what the night time is for.


(* The last line is from a letter Monroe wrote
    to her psychiatrist in 1961.)

# Doris Day

American actress, singer, activist

     i.m.   (her voice)

The toll life makes you pay
I won't begrudge, since that's
what makes it worth living,
not for a song, mind you,
but for a belonging sense
that animals, yes, are born
and die with, as the teachers
they are. The star I was lucky
to be born under carried me far,
but the truth is, dogs-cum-husbands
were the ruin of me. That's why
I prefer the company of true dogs
that I care for, who shoulder
the world's pain without an iota
of resentment—they don't hunger
for anything but kindness, a show
that's our real business, after all
is said and done, as per animal
instinct that makes us most human.

# Tom Hanks

American actor, filmmaker

(his voice)   —after *Forrest Gump*, dir. Robert Zemeckis

The box of chocolates life is
(without ever knowing what you'll get)
tastes good to he or she who eats it
one at a time, while the whole shebang
is out of your control. So sayeth the
soothsayer in the wisdom of
his ears. We have traveled the length
and breadth of the United States to
tell our story, one of miscues tied
to cliches hooked to the stars, and
I follow the train of thought leading
to the love of my life and back again.
It's how I've learned to live with
myself, for the world to mean to me.
She, the world, is all I have now.
I'll tell her story when I can.
In the meantime I'll have the next
piece of chocolate, minus a plan.

# Robin Williams

American actor, comedian i.m.

(his voice)  —after a YouTube interview

I sold my soul to the devil
in me, or would have if I
could have found it—my
soul that is. For the last time
I looked I could see my body
getting on in years, forced
to its knees, with my
fears not fully faced and
ten thousand voices to sound
out the world that played
its joke on me. It's laughable
how a man'll do anything
to not die but stay afloat
on the sea of mirrors where,
upon reflection, I lose myself
abysmally each time out. And
believe me, no smile can tile
the floor I would want to walk
on, the house I've lived in all
my life a stranger's haven,
heavenly bones stored away
on its father shore of sorrow
where my soul has gone today
and where, as per my manic talk,
I guess I'll do stand-up tomorrow.

# Bill Maher

American comedian

(his voice)  2011

America, once great, had a strange fate.
We let it go down the tubes
with the Repubs at the helm.
Now we got a king of the realm
to look up to, us whities.
Did I mention he's black?
No, I'm not racist, just sayin'.
What our future looks like
is anybody's guess. But we'd
better stop saying no to Love's yes.
The power trip we've been on
will run us into the ground.
It's time to re-imagine ideals,
not just kill to close deals.
Let's hear you say, We love U.S.A.!
Say it loud, say it proud,
before it gets said by the shroud.

# Bill Murray

American actor

(his voice)   —after *Groundhog Day*, dir. Harold Ramis

The beat we now walk repeats ad infinitum
(or so it seems)...You didn't come here
to swing like a goofball.
Be in production & partnership with the Other.
(He ratifies new laws under his jurisdiction.)
Get up & fulfill yourself. Don't push back
against the wind, go with the flow. Anxious
Nowheresville you inhabit will dissolve into
a fresh scene if you can make it happen, and
be there wholeheartedly, with your mind on
full alert, the new life closer than you think.

# Stephen Colbert

American comedian

(his voice) 2015

In twerp heaven, I shine.
It's what I do walking the line
between fodder for idiots and
mulch for maniacs. I
fit comfortably to balance
the country's follies and foibles
and the retards on the right,
and make my points tight.
It's a drag I won't take
on Puff the Magic Dragon's time.
They know—my audience does—
where I'm coming from, but nobody
—not even me—knows where I'm going.
That's the fun of it. A nine-year
run isn't half bad in character.
Now I'm in search of a new
plotline to inhabit, to plot
my next course. It's intellectual
locomotion I get a rush out of.
Here's to the choo-choo I
climb aboard next time!
Hoist the pirate flag up the pole
until I can play a new role!
It's what I do to save my soul.

# Jerry Seinfeld

American comedian

(his voice) —after an episode, with Garry Sandling, of
                      *Comedians in Cars Getting Coffee,* 2016

Here in L.A. where all the best
comics came for the best T & A,
the coke-snorting tribe who scored
the best drugs in town, all came
here to crash and burn, and you
were the best of that tribe, admit
it. We're on TV so you can only
admit so much, but Goofy here
is a soft touch, and hey! What
won't bite back will kick my
ratings into high gear! Fuck 'em!
I say. No, not him, but nay-sayers
who get on my case for my show.
I'm Jerry, you're not. Fuck you!
Let's roll and rock some fun. Time
flies when you're in a Porsche.
The Rorschach test of a comic's
psyche we do, is usually spot on.
So stick around as I throttle my
schtick for a few laughs, sans
toupee, the both of us. But con-
cocting what's cocked in both of
us on live TV, with a 15-second delay
for improved editing. Right? Right.
Now scram! Get outta here!

# Carrie Fisher

American actress, author


i.m. 2016   (her voice)


I died a long time ago folks but I lived
to tell the tale, many times over and
under the 'Star Wars' banner I was lucky
to hoist up as I went, day by day a bitch
and a half, make no mistake, Hollywood
child that I was. It was no picnic, I can
tell you, and I did. That's what made
my life worth living—the telling of it.
Hear me now, from the other side, there's
no other life but this one, it's up to you
to live yours as best you can. May the Force
be with you always. Do I have any last
words to top those? Don't let my light go out…
…You're right, you're right. I know you're right.

# Dave Chappelle

American stand-up comedian

(his voice)

Reefer don't pay for the blind man running
around on stage but it sure enough makes him
sing. So sing I will. …Hey, brother, what gives?
You sitting there think you know me? Let me
tell you who I am. I got the shakes from living
my life in the open, but you, you can duck
for cover and still not know who you are!
I'm telling you that the mouth has an engine
all its own, and it runs non-stop with stories
I can tell you that would blow your mind.

# Jarett Kobek

Turkish-American writer

(his voice)

It's time to blow the wad of the Patriarchy
and be rid of it once and for all, and that's
what the Internet and celebrity culture will,
in the long run, accomplish: take down the
Patriarchy by the very same tools that are
propping it up. There's no point in waiting
for it to happen, though—it's time to make
it happen, the sooner the better! We've gunned
our culture into wise-ass territory where,
it's true, I'm cleaning up (hey, I'm no saint!).
But deep down my instincts are: don't stick it
to your friends, a Mafia credo if ever there
was one. But I'm speaking Greek here—
Epicurean… cure-all for our capitalist culture?

# Joe Zimmerman

American stand-up comedian

(his voice) circa 2016

We stage the jokes to fit the times
we're living, but cosmic space has
the edge for me, given the elephant
in the room we'd do better to avoid.
I hear claims from the audience,
beer-wise, but that won't go over
past the moment. In your face is
not a place worth going to, it's without
legs. I prefer to open up the body
politic with inner light of my own.
The mapless territory the mind takes
up as it goes along, makes the unknown.

# Part Three

*Looking out at what
the sky is full of—
stars and more stars.*

# Oleg Cricket

Russian extreme stuntman

(his voice)

Barefoot in the abyss, the soul-body
conundrum, believe me, is more terrible
for being close to the bone. Becoming
one with my aloneness, however, is
more fun than I can say. Look with me
into the depths and I'll take you on
the ride of your life. Just don't die
on me, is what I hear all the time.
That thought, when it crosses the transom
of my mind, makes me dizzier than does
the swag I show on every ledge I go out
on. The (extreme) stunts I pull, push me
to the max. Let limits sleep, no lie.
Every dude wants fame, and a name
to lift him higher. Where I go, I dare
you to follow. This is no game. Reasons
I can't give is my only reason for living,
meaning: let's play hard, be stronger,
working it clean of our fear of falling.
Let it all be seen by the doctor of my soul,
this aerial view, this selfie in the abyss,
this going out on a limb of the tree of life.

# Anthony T. Kronman

American law professor, author

(his voice)  —after *Confessions of a Born-Again Pagan*

The god we go at in words
is gorgeous beyond belief—
this the poets tell us is true
demonstrably, falsehoods et al.
We philosophize on this matter
to materialize the forms anew,
a god-like power to be sure.
What looks betray, books portray
in myriad lines of sight.
A blinding flash of light replays
it over and over again each night
that no amen can finalize. Love
comes not into play without knowledge
of itself, so we bank on it to say
for us what it can and cannot be,
or do. Either way we are beholden
to what gets old for being told, thus
time is born, and reborn in us
as rhyme we hear eternally—
fleshed out in the space of language
we learn by the stars to see.
Give us this daily bread what imagination
only half bakes, the wholesome deity
says, and the rest will be revealed
to you in view of one's corporate duty

to the sphere political-cum-personal,
the body dreamed of as it radically seems—
as real to the touch as words are, and
as golden as the sun on high shining over all.

# Mark Patrick Hederman

Irish contemplative writer

(his voice)

i

Abstruse conjurations we abjure, to seek
instead, concrete contemplation of the darkness,
for what? for counsel and documentation
of a future hopefully far-reaching and freeing.

ii

Take mythic aim at your beast:
what's in your sights by your third eye
is your underworld self's version of
who you are or have been marked as.
But banging your head against the mob's
opinion of you would only destroy you;
better to walk away and ignore their jeers,
preserving your vision for another day.

iii

The artist forges new links between
the visible and invisible realms through
which flows energy newly released
and transformed in the recipient, called
the artistic experience, whether in

the language of film, painting, sculpture,
fiction, poetry, drama or what have you.
The question for us, humbly asked, is
how to harness this energy for society at large.

iv

When in here inheres out there
where out there inheres in here,
hero of both, hero of neither,
be stillness in motion,
a particle waving at emotion.

Here where the nameless reside,
the flowers bloom, the petals
burst forth. Here where the nameless
reside, the raindrops thicken
the soil washed clean of the sounding
call, the metaphysical desire to mean,
and the well at the source is a fountain
whose arising out of depths turns
the surface one way, then another
as movement we die into
for the stillness we love.

# Karl Ove Knausgård

Norwegian author

(his voice)

i

You can't do a thing that grievous.
The clowns we were made sure of that.
Musicians we were, in name only,
and our first gig being a fiasco
only solidifies that fact for us.

You showed me your underwear.
How could you do a thing like that?
This is your gift to the world.

ii  after an interview

For a man of the world, he brings
along with him a very active
imagination. Little escapes his
notice. His painter's eye is alert
to form and color. You can feel
he's madly in love with words,
with the formal properties and
expressive potential of language.
He's wired to the world from
the top of his head to his toes.
He takes seriously the role of

writer, the way often Europeans
do. He seems to delight in
the life of travel and meeting
important writers whom he respects,
to engage them and stake out
new ground with them.
His interviewer took very little
from him: what you know and
what you want to share renders
him autonomous as he digs his own
life and travels the world for answers.

# Bob Dylan

American singer-songwriter

—after "Murder Most Foul," 2020

He sings the things of the soul
America lost, to try to stay whole.
He writes the only anthem
he can, between us and them.
He holds up a candle to the picture
of the past, but where's the future,
he asks. The countdown starts
where the doomsday clock imparts
its message that nobody hears—
time runs out with human fears.
He pierces the veil of history
to bleed out its mystery.
He bandages our wound
by a piano lovingly tuned.
He gives voice to the darkness
we inhabit, regardless.
He toys with the phrases
while turning the pages
he wrote in the night.
If only… it could make things right.

# Leonard Cohen

Canadian singer-songwriter

(his voice)

The world that we create
with our love and our hate
…how can I say that?
it sounds so trite…
the world that we create
with our love and our hate
…I can't get the thought
out of my mind, its little feet…
the world that we create
with our love and our hate
… is a song without end
that takes my hand.

# Leonard Cohen & Bob Dylan

i

Cohen

Whaddya have to ease
the pain of compassion?
he said, wincing.

Dylan

I have leftover elation,
he said, grimacing,
but won't aim to please.


ii  song w/ missing line sung by Cohen in a dream

I lived in the dream of the moment
and between earth and I
everywhere I went
eternity shone its light.
[ .... ]
and died out of sight
to make my wrongs aright.

A thousand ephemeral answers
for every timeless question
keeps me busy thinking
up words and sentences
to put them in.

# Linkin Park

American rock band

(their voices)   —after *A Thousand Suns*

Let the mushroom cloud disperse
in the brain's alternate universe
and hear shatter those idols
of the past, the voice's newest cycles
to emerge from the historical record
that touches a human chord,
saying We, a David, smite the State's
Goliath stranglehold on the fates
of millions, and raise up individual
conscience's sword to fight all
enemy wolves in sheep's clothing.
So let our notes run riot, and sing.

# Ralph Vaughn Williams

English composer

(his voice)

My Ariel and my Falstaff dialogued throughout
my life, heaving symphonies and choral
works into the public ear, while
through my myriad relations with women ran
a passion for beauty and youth that sustained
my spirit and fueled my calling to music.
Is there no better way to touch others than
to allow yourself to be touched? Largeness
of the man I was and largeness of the vision
I celebrated kept me focused, but Blake's Job
went further and opened doors to a new orbit,
called Ursula, my muse until my dying day,
she who wedded me to a living song.

# Sudo Genki

Japanese pro wrestler, politician

(his voice)

Time in the fourth dimension
conquers all, or has the will to,
the same thing in my mind. The here
and now I place bets on, to press
home what I mean, and am.
Selfish I was, to a fault. Forget
me not, I insisted, and fought
to make it happen. Strife and
heartbreak, for all the pain, make
for a more interesting world. I say
re-order it with all you have,
with kindness and self-control.
It's a bargain I'll keep my end of.
Call it, if you like, Japanese love.

# Julian Jaynes

American psychology researcher, author

—after *The Origin of Consciousness in the Breakdown
of the Bicameral Mind*

i    (his voice)

Spatialized time is the only time there is,
our only experience of it before and after.
In a mind-space where memory, a flame
undying as long as we can access it, is born.
Once our mind-space is closed off, memory dies.
Personal memory, that is. But suppose
a poem, once read by you, achieves a place
in your memory that outlives the poet, his words
continuing to resonate in your mind-space as
a step toward immmortality that poets seek.
(Even slips of the tongue can help point the way…)
But even after his words are 'imported' into your
mind-space they can just as easily be forgotten
by, say, atrophy, or neglect, or plain forgetfulness,
which is to say, suffer a lack of quotation.
Now we have entered territory of the text
where we are bound by the law of Logos.
How the poet authorizes the poem into being so as
to obey that law and also to live long in a
readership which, hopefully, will give his words
new life, is at issue here, touching on deeper
mysteries of story-telling and narration…

ii


…Julian Jaynes moves the stars
and the heavens into a position
where we can see ourselves
more clearly under them as
once-unconscious humans now
conscious of our world and
our places in it. He entered
the fray with a theory of the ages.


Song-sweet
come cry


fit the prize
for landing true


here as history
of bloody Babylon.



The what-next of death is all there is
left of the I of the beholder, consciousness
gone the way of conversation, like this,
in passing. Going went gone into space
without time to waste, a plenum, a bliss.

# Kendrick Lamar

American rapper

(his voice) —after a music video

Wingbeats of a pimped butterfly
fill my ears and raise the sky
from down here where it resonates:

Young man, would you like to come with me?
The warning I'll issue this time is for your benefit.
Next time it'll be a helluva lot worse.
Take my word for it young man—
Hell is no place you want to know.

# Rihanna

Barbadian singer

(her voice) —after a music video

Come join me sometime.
You can be my dick.

That's very allowable.
It's got punch and sass.

Add a twist of venom
and we've nailed it!

What is it if not
the soul's glamour?

Darkness & [    ]
in an age of impermanent desire.

# Simon Cowell

English TV personality

(his voice)  —after *American Idol*

Beautiful undies to flash the TV audience with,
will take you far. Don't get me wrong, you're
already a star. We make 'em or break 'em.
But when they're made, we stand back in awe.
You're at the pinnacle of the wave that brought
you here to this stage, and wow what a message
you bring all wannabe stars in your wake.

# Claire Danes

American actress

—after *Homeland*

'Carrie' dangles over the edge to see
how far she would dare the abyss
to take her as she is, a woman bared
for the world to see. She defends her
right to decide for herself, and does
whatever's necessary, snap decisions
grunt work, second-guessing, the
works, and she falls nine times out
of ten and still gets back up to show
her teeth, her eyes flashing, her
pride bristling, her skin sweating.
What woman is this, with scorn
to guide her steps towards love
which she embraces in her arms,
fitfully, a cocktease who henpecks
compatriots until she gets her way.

# Linda Blair

American actress

—after *The Exorcist,* dir. William Friedkin

She possessed an evil that possessed her
when goodness drew near, making clear
it was death she had to hold dear, ice cold
down to her fingers and toes, the breath
inverted to show the other realm's space
we occupy unknowingly, innocent of
what can be cast out in the end, by facing
one's fear head on, to the dead and forward,
not going back again having come this far,
unclear if that house is ever left for good.

# Coco Vandeweghe

American pro tennis player

(her voice)   —after the Australian Open, 2017

Times we live in a woman rhymes
with power, to the extent she takes
it, and I intend to take what's mine
if I have to fight for it with every
breath and, in my case, racket stroke.
I'll bang on every closed door and
wrestle every point to the floor to
get my due, and no one will stand
in my way if I have any say. She—
my opponent—will not be given any
free points but will have to earn them.
Meanwhile I burn with fires deep
inside me that I'll warm my life by
one game, one match at a time.

# Roger Federer & Rafael Nadal

i  R.F. (his voice)

The clockwork I play like,
with a stick that talks, earns
me accolades and more money
than I know what to do with.
The trouble is, the clock will
run down, then what'll I do?
The back burner that thought's
on keeps me awake at night,
thinking thoughts between
myself, the moon, and the stars.


ii  R.N. (his voice)

Yes, the energy Roger has
to play the game he loves
is mind-boggling. I've won
more matches than I've lost
against him, however, which
makes our rivalry a good one.
I don't know but I hope it keeps
going while I have energy
of my own to peek into the future.
And what do I see him doing?
A TV personality, maybe, or
a popular politician a la
Arnold Schwarzenegger.

Either way, he'll stay
in Europe, I'm pretty sure.
The crowds messed up my hair,
the parts the wind didn't mess up.
It's a problem for a balding guy
like me, who wants to hide
his baldness at any cost.
I have a proud tongue,
but I understand that heart.

# The Bryan Brothers

—American pro tennis players

Each playing doubles
at the highest levels,
spanning the dry depths
of autonomy and the sticky
heights of camaraderie, both
shining in their athletic dance
of Tweedledee and Tweedledum,
Mike and Bob, playing
to close out the match.

# Meredith Sabini

American Jungian writer

(her voice)

Do you want to dream your
life away? Of course not.
Do you want to dream your
way into new fields of
vision and experience? Then
it's time you woke up
to the potentialities of your
dreamlife. But know this:
The work it involves requires
that you go slow. Liminal
spaces are accessed via trance
and meditation techniques.
Such knowledge as it may
yield may also lead into
unsafe areas for which
in order to cope when facing
real risks and dangers,
one needs training.

# The Risk

Whatever psychic leverage
might be gained in dreams
or in tapping the collective
unconscious that dreamlife
represents, is lost from
having to counterbalance the swing
towards the primitive or primordial
mind, with the swing
back towards the civilized mind
and rational control.
Both mindsets exert their power
over the poet, and both
require energy to bring their power
to bear in one's writing.
Such creative energies as are
called up in this process
cannot be predicted, let alone
controlled. There is no way
of knowing beforehand if one
will or will not be led over
the psychic cliff, but it is a risk
that one must take. A ritual
courtship ensues between the poet
and his muse—for the benefit of
the child of that marriage, so to speak.
There is no guarantee, however,
that the forces unleashed from
this union won't destroy the artist.
Every working artist knows this, and

if properly trained, makes provisions
for the inevitable consequences, either
anticipated or unanticipated,
of this fated union.


*


…I hear him listening to us.

What does he sound like?

A gun before going off.
A shallow grave.
An unguarded moment.
A godless prayer.

As an underground witness, what
does he hear?

Time softening
into space.
Wheels turning
backwards.
Infinitesimally small
beginnings.
Dolor undying.
Hands reaching
the next rung
on the ladder
of being.
Shadows needing
walls.

# Part Four

*He sets the bar high*
*for unclaimed stars.*

# On Some American Poets

i  William Carlos Williams


(late summer and all)


I have days ahead of me
that look back at what I got
wrong, which will be much,
but also, at what I got right,
a touch of madness guiding
me there, on the back of a hunch,
and though it's not a winning
formula, it's enough, my fill
of wasted words notwithstanding,
that some roots will have taken,
will have gripped down
and begun to awaken.


ii  Sylvia Plath


Condemned to be damning
of the pyre she set herself
upon, as an act of self-
immolation undertaken early
on, to be lately accomplished,
the wished-for death ascribed
to a fatherlessness that haunted
her lines, poetry's and life's, a drama
husband-multiplied until what

sustained her fell away,
so she lit a perfect flame
that would carry her
into fame.


iii   Robert Lowell


The poet whom I thought fire
turned out to be
water, or the startled fish     swimming
through it like some preternatural god
or aboriginal being, one ill-advised
to reveal itself to those of us
inclined to violence, to judgement,
to language.
                    Still, he rose
out of the gun-metal sea long enough
to invent the shore before
vanishing into the circle of
possession, his and ours, no circle
without the distant roar of surf breaking
(as another poet has said), heard
in the first but only night
that, ignited, we lit with stars.


iv   Frank O'Hara


Frank O'Hara does for culture
what Mary Oliver does for nature—
crowds words onto pages
in the name of everyday sublimity.

He died on the day
the dunes deflected
the light in the middle
of the darkness.


v   Bob Kaufman


   (his voice)


Going down in
history to be
hidden away


in time.


vi  Richard Wilbur


   (his voice)


My imposter self loaded up on
rhythms and syllables, to make
its way through the fake woods
my decadence had conjured, true
to form, out of a poetic nothing,
rhythmic grace punctuated by
the ameliorations of memory,
like swans that would lift into
air, winging somewhere far
from despair. Call it wonder.
Even as the next heart hardens from
artlessness it seeks to overcome.

vii   Robert Bly  i.m.


   (his voice)


I see where the gods go
hungry and looking for
their next meal of the ego
hunt that is their lives



viii   Jack Gilbert


   (his voice)


You'll never find me
in my poems, though
I wrote them to be found.
Is there any other way?



ix   Richard Howard   i.m.


You can't say guano
on the street
You can't say crazy
without the heat


There's no saying why I
would do it, I just think
I would.


There aren't too many of us.

The sunset he rides off in
makes dawn all the more precious.

A specialist, right?

Look, can I start by backing up?
Richard Howard knows a ton of shit.


xx  Audre Lorde

What she bore witness to
is what she embodied—
Black woman on the rise


xi  Joseph Brodsky

I've almost stopped dreaming about you
but the articles about your life I reread
tumble with verbs: reviled, persecuted,
condemned, imprisoned, released,
emigrated, settled, taught, wrote,
published, translated, won, praised—
now all adjectives in the past tense
holding you in the amber of time.


xii  Sharon Olds

  (her voice)

Fruit jars on the counter resemble the scientific
experiment made of the carefully observed.

A bond made for the future fling modeled
after ones among us who're most like creatures.
More than that, to be quite honest, you must take on
the flight and its headway to make it all worthwhile.
(You are the perfection in me. I could feel you
all grained and ad hoc, impromptu as Americans tend to do.)


xiii  Philip Schultz


    —after a YouTube video, 2018


He winces not from pain
but from awkwardness
at standing in front of
an audience and reading aloud
his poems, some for the first
time, the wise words he would never
admit to their being
rising in the space he only makes bigger,
mesmerizing, hospitable, adulterated.
But the pain his poems evince
permits life:
making a deal with mortality, he calls it.


xiv  Joy Harjo


    (her voice)  —after *Our Songs Came Through,* Ed.


It is time you heard our voices
in the fullness of time, not as Native
nor as American but as inhabitants

of sacred lands we've always been
a part of. It is time we constituted,
in the music of our forefathers and
foremothers, a new melody that
will be heard for generations to come.
It is time our DNA is woven in the strand
of what it means to be alive, human,
and remembered, poetry by any other name.
It is time, it is time, it is time.


xv  Adam Zagajewski  i.m.


the whole apparatus,
the whole structure of things
lies in tatters around us
yet the poet brings
back a certain sense
of what it once was,
in verse without pretense,
nor to much applause.
but now it's grown late
and he has gone,
so why wait?...
we're already alone.


xvi  Li-Young Lee


(his voice)


Fire rages in my art
to burn up the cages in my heart—

let its heat arm the reader
against the violence of the world,
and may its ash to come
soften the blows of beauty
that is born of the unsaid.


xvii   Jennifer Barber

   —after *The Sliding Boat Our Bodies Made*

Not this winter, nor the next,
nor the one after that, but
the one that lasts, is what
she contemplates in the evening
before bed, and in the morning
in the bed she will rise from.


xviii  Amy King

   (her voice)

So ruin came, unstoppable,
into the life of Europe,
and Hitler drowned us all
in the bloodlust of his music.
He became architect of a future
that burned its way into
the consciousness, the heat
of his will ablaze with destruction.

We worshipped the divine in
the candleflame
before it got snuffed out.

By what?

By history's version of history.


xix  Judy Halebsky

(her voice) —after *Spring and a Thousand Years*
*(Unabridged)*

Americans don't listen because
everyone wants to be heard
above the din of all the voices
non-stop without saying a word
to the wise talking talking talking
past the sound, the silence of grief.


xx  Antler

(his voice)

The pot to piss in we poets don't have
puts the ear on call—listen to us, hear
our woke words for all, spoken in love,
and perfect harmony will greet the seer
to come, the one we are waiting for,
the one who'll be writing with nerve
by taking the pulse of love's body
to save secrets it alone knows.

# Diane Seuss

American poet

i   —after an interview w/ Daniel Drake

She hails the taxi to doom and bows
when she arrives, to whomever would
greet her, the brow wet with anticipation,
the hair mussed from the effort of reaching
her destination, her poetic target rounded
off by one line after another until the end,
modern for being what Being presses her
to be, no guesswork from here on in, or out.

ii     —after *frank:sonnets*

A 22-year-old wannabe rapper shoots up a July 4th
parade in Illinois on the day I dive into her sonnets
up to my knees in her memories her roundabout
wayward past now up to my neck in it I can barely
make out where she's headed next she has us all
guessing the 14-line singing she does across the page
all the rage I've heard so I bought into her rage
for the lowdown she falls into and floats across
to the laugh lines coke lines who knows I don't
mind either way she is no James Merrill and is
loved for it a working-class heroine in the sun
making of a soul's foul weather some harsh bit of fun.

# Garret Hongo

Japanese American poet

(his voice)

Who are these people?
(Do or say what they will,
I done said my fill…)
It's a hootenanny out there
in the poetry world, everybody
dancing with everybody else
amid musics that go on into the night
on and on into a light that makes us all shine
And I'm fine with it the shadows too have a way with words

These days a lotta talented kids
out there, but they gotta whore.
It's a hard row to hoe that's for sure,
no matter who you think you are.
Time weeds out those without a muse
to stick by them through thick and thin.
The chaff from the wheat duly separated
leaves a handful whose voices get heard.
I won't pretend to know the whys,
wherefores and hows, but to this process
I have no choice but to bow. It, not me,
turns the gears of the monkey grinder,
and we so-called poets for the culture at large
are tolerated, hardly celebrated, mostly aggravated
into dissing our brothers & sisters in Poetry

to get what we think's our fair share
of fame, recognition, name—slim pickings all.
But that's the game & them's the rules
we set out to master
with the aim of outlasting all comers
at whatever the cost to ourselves.

So, see you on the narrow road of the Poetic!
where no critter wants to be runt of the litter,
but we poets, we know no other way.
Lord knows how we've clawed tooth and nail
just to be able to say: I've had my say!
And a better day is not coming before night
swallows us whole, in cold delight.
You want heat to warm your cockles by,
find another beat! Either way, you die
a thousand deaths before learning why
and how life's the school in which one learns
staying open to this drama of humankind
takes you to what you need to find.

# Franz Wright

American poet    i.m. 2015

(his voice)

I've had problems. Read me
and find out.


The puppy-dogs and milquetoasts of this world
will, as we know from bitter experience, get crushed
under cruelty's thumb, but no tears will be spilled
by me, so forewarned is, as they say, forearmed.
We won't waste any more words. Let silence
be broken once and for all, for what's damning
is knowing the truth (of evil) and not raising
your voice against it. It's what I do, poet-wise,
that I've earned the right to after all these years,
walking and talking my way into the annals
of "loose canon"—yes we can! And did!
Who says we can't say what needs undamning,
when undamning's called for? The ace of spades
I got dealt is no king of hearts, so I'll play
what's on the table on my own terms and
by my own wits. I grieve for my own pending death
but won't reveal the ace up my sleeve.
Poker-faced I've learned to be, and
I've played with the best of them.
It's my shots I call, not theirs!
I got lots of other tricks, too. Stay tuned.

*

The oral engine
that keeps everything
going: FW
Meanwhile, love is
propped up against your
gravestone.

*

It's returns that make people happy.

Happy? It makes them hard.

Notes I'll no, day by day,
under the yes they hold up,
invisible melody of my
soul, heard in a vision
of maybe… maybe I did
the evil to myself and now
I know it. But
only by saying
I live in the greatness
of my death
to hear the everlasting
music of now.
Well come.

Make the sale of
your tale the whale
you're in the belly of!

Look at books,
you see them
classics of death
everyday
as the made and arrayed
pages tell it.

The way the world
sees itself
is built of words—a house of cards?—
the way the world is,
is made of love
from a house of bards

Nature's sweeping destructiveness
death de-constructs
for love's
constructiveness—
where what is sharp
can be blunt
and what is heart-shaped
is a cunt.
May the penis of us
make room for
both Venus and Mars
to learn to celebrate
scars of heaven
as well as stars
of hell.

*

They've just lowered its prestige, the poet
laureate, which never should be given
to begin with, but if necessary, give it
to a real artist whose life and work
embody the values of the artist at his
or her best, not trifling MFA programs
and deceiving students mindlessly of
their supposed 'genius.' What a phony
honor if ever there was one! But hey,
had I a chance at it I'd have a laugh
at its expense, so help me god! I'd say
what you—the rest of you—only dream
of saying, and I'd tell it true, too,
loud and clear for all to hear, how
bankrupting the artistic life with fake
honors undermines the role the artist
plays, must play, at the edges of society
where they belong. No poet, no self-respecting
poet would deign accept the post of poet
laureate now made trivial by its newest
occupant. But who's naming names? Not
me! I won't waste my bile to attack one
so unworthy. Cold my heart feels at the
injustice and neglect, but so be it. None
but the brave weather storms such as I've
weathered, which as you can see have
re-shaped my face monumentally, a nature-
carved man am I. Let it—my face—be my
glory earned, the truth of it burned onto the
retinas of all who'd look upon me. I am my
own starry-eyed monster and make no bones

except to raise a cry on behalf of poetry
which I revere and serve faithfully, and will
do so until my dying day. May the snot-nosed
poet wannabes take note: charged and charred
by lightning from hell is all that he—the grim-
faced one—ever wrote! Read his work with
all due caution, then, and at your own risk,
the poetry I'll live and die by, not the drivel
society seems to prize. Let others better
or more deserving than I agree. But please
don't foist upon me or the sleeping world
anything less than the real deal, he or she
I'd go to the mats for, I'd croon for not sneer
at, as I would at the likes of the latest 'chosen one'
whose light burns on ambition's throne
to render poetry more alone, more detached
than ever before.


*


Yes, you have suffered greatly
in your life
but nothing like the joys
you have felt.
In either or both cases
by your sharing them—the joys and sufferings—
meaning was made,
and for that you wish only
to offer in return your
undying gratitude.

# Miho Nonaka

Japanese expatriate poet and translator

(her voice)

Too precious for words, too good to be true,
too 'pure' and I'm unsure if the tag we played
today on the playground of our minds wasn't
rigged in your favor, it's the way of the world
and I'm not one to change its terms. But let's be
firm in our resident feelings for the injustice
of it all, me in America, me who in her heart—
"right place" or not—knows the terms as stacked
against me, a female, a Japanese one at that, in
a landscape men control. It's not your fault
and I'm not suggesting it is, but with God's
silence as my witness, the rage I have I can't
rave about in your presence, save in Morse code—
the lifting eyelids, the dense particulars of
a maverick intelligence, or a heart that won't tolerate
what it's been forced to feed on, religion be damned,
global potential too! We sit together and our eyes
meet as windows the soul gives us to look out
onto a soulless world, were you to know it as
I do, for all your positive talk. The walk we take
is the ache History stalks sisters by—brotherhood's
true face. Scary it is, and conflicted, perilous with
pain unapproachable by the mind that would
comprehend it. I am satisfied by nothing so much as
justice I know I won't ever see in my lifetime,

but it's what lights *my* fire, where love—and
its expansive ilk—skies the ocean with clouds
that block my view of the sun. Pretty lame,
isn't it, what a culture of Names adds up to,
but we're stuck with it, with all due respect—
and I'll pray to a god of silence to set things
right, knowing they never will be. Faith?
I have none. Trust me, Death wins every time:
One says "Dickinson," another says "Whitman,"
and you Americans think the world owes you
thanks in perpetuity. Well, let me thank you
with bows and scrapes galore, for all that your
folklore can do… Hard-nosed is hard-hearted
is hard-assed, I know all about that, and more.

# Shuntaro Tanikawa

Japanese poet


The shit-stirring potential of these poems of his
leaves a stench on my fingers. Hold that dream.


*


The fame-chaser found what he was looking for,
and it revolted him to no end. This has no end.


*


Lines of inspiration would keep coming
no matter if he turned off the spigot. The page.


*


I won't begrudge the blessings bestowed upon
your name, he said, forgetting who he was talking to.


*


Time for him held out the possibility
of no time. That kept for him the mirror polished.

# John Ashbery

American poet

i    a cento  (composed of and inspired by J.A. poem titles)

Purists will object… we hesitate… but
something similar—here
(in the absence of a noble presence
where everything is still floating)
is another chain letter.
The ongoing story is just walking around
as we know, in pursuit of happiness.
Some words, some trees, some old tires,
a last world's blessing in disguise.
And you know the young son, a boy
—the Pied Piper of popular songs—
through the grapevine hears
thoughts of a young girl
("How much longer will I be able
to inhabit the divine sepulcher…")
whose white roses conjure our youth,
the songs we know best.
But for now, the recent past many wagons ago
(last month to be exact) (saying it
to keep it from happening) utters
unctuous platitudes, paradoxes, and oxymorons
with or without a qualm. (Thank you for not cooperating.)
Friends— my erotic doubles, I'd love
you to be in it, the plural of "Jack-in-the-box",
like the couple in the next room—meanwhile

are vaguer presences in this configuration, past
the ice-cream wars of the Other Tradition,
which turns like this late echo
into a haunted landscape of flowering death.
Oh if the birds knew
what a self-portrait in a convex mirror really was! How
it's a decoy of mixed feelings, a plainness
in diversity that is the grand
gallop of a task! How
whatever it is—silhouette, tapestry, crazy weather, or rivers
and mountains; wherever you are—spring day, bungalows
on the towpath, wooden buildings, or the ivory tower—
it's (also)
a  wave.


ii


Having found my way inside
I couldn't if I tried
come out again into
the light where the sun
shone on everyone but me.
I thanked my lucky stars, however,
for the discovery
of my light under the bushel
I prayed would last.
not top drawer, mind you,
but within reach
of you

as I let the shadows
fall away
where shining bright

in the sky is the moon
in the darkness
as clouds rush past.

*

The pain you thought you outlasted
remains, part of the past, part
of the future,

the present enlarged
by the presence of the sun.

*

We rise in hardness to the skies
before the distant sun in us dies,
as winterized down to our roots
we sing our moral substitutes.

*

just sitting in the sun
gets the job done.

*

The sun shines down
on us all, he says.

Except for when the clouds
get in the way.

Sunshine on a cloudy day
makes the ghosts go away.

*

I think I'll sit here and
look at the moon a while.

…We have a moon and
we have a sun.

My god who came up
with that one!...

It's dropping between
the branches of a tree

visible against the darkness,
ever more real

for being a mystery
to me.

*

The pictured reflection evaporates into a pause,
a peripheral visage peering out at it—
the sun—as if a born star, radiant
beyond recognition, and as unignorably exact.

Late and dark the time had come
to a place where to write was to fall
hard for the sound you would hear

at the end of the day with the news all
but told and the bed all but slept in
not an hour too soon nor dawn too light
while the poet in you sees a strange thing
and holds it high and close as the sun.

# Eileen Myles

American poet

(her voice)

On your feet, no more lying
about in your bed of dreams.
What's real, hero, beckons you to feel
the heartbeat in the face of death—
boom boom, boom boom—or is it
a crack of lightning before
the thunder roars.


*


Hit the deck
Save your neck
She who's awake
will live to see
the wreck
of History.


*


Human beings are the authorities
of their own stories they live.


*


Autonomy reflects well
on those who have it,

or want it. The darkest part
of it lies within, however,
where everything depends,
and depends wholly,
on every other part.


*


a hurricane of lies in whose vortex
sucked down whirling into its eye
is the truth of your poem
yet to be written

# Rainer Marie Rilke

Austrian poet

i  Auguste Rodin

We wouldn't have the profundities
he excavated preternaturally
had it not been for Rodin, he who infused
the poet's lines with energy all-consuming,
a relentlessly churning practice poetry
came to mean for the poet, a working
philosophy that allowed him to spread
his wings and in unearthly relation
plunge into the Holy—
that caged Earth thrown off
for the emptiness he felt at home in.

ii  Louise Gluck

Pouring Rilke through an American sieve
conceives
immaculately what one might have thought
was his alone
as a trace of transformation leaves
a memory we keep having
to have—
how finely wrought
her lines and natural her tone
in having her fill
of his beautiful
autumnal moon.

iii


Look, if anyone can live the angelic
it's Rilke.

# Kate Daniels

American poet, memoirist

—after *Slow Fuse of the Possible*

i

Before you read another word
of her memoir about poetry
and psychoanalysis you search
for her poems online to see how,
as it were, her mind works,
which, to your mind at least,
only poems can reveal, prose
being a hideout of sorts, not
the temporary kind, as poems
are or can be, poetry being
that place where the mind can't
help but be, not at one with
itself (can it ever be?), nor
at peace with itself (far from it),
nor exactly at odds with itself
or with the world (conflict
being too strong a word?), but
somehow at home, every word
or line a release of salient
or sanative or operative
human longing to tell, even
at a remove, its tale when—
especially when— the well

gone to is a replenishing
of the ending deferred to another day,
the adjectives for her despair
meanwhile, holding the tale up.


ii (her voice)


She slayed my understanding, took it away
piece by piece into the mind at play.
When eyeball to eyeball, we add a crumb
of intimacy to the sum of human relationship
we are building together in that room,
a womb for a second birth, if it comes,
I'm longingly there for — the room full
of poems, the poems full of stanzas,
a mirroring in which we can see
ourselves startlingly clearly. The mind opens
and images fall into it, even as
we ourselves fall into the images.

# Lisa Hiton

American poet


—after "The Senator"


She dares the dream to envelope her
and send her on her way into reality
transformed, but it gets more real
than she expected, the gun that is
not a gun loaded with real bullets
fired at a target moving faster than
the heart it's aimed at, hers or ours,
it doesn't make any difference now.
Space timed to a different beat, and
memory's prayer shawl wrapping
itself around her shoulders for
comfort it will not give, together
make a story she will relive over
and over again until the words
she utters in the poem free her
from the nightmare she died in.

# Kathy Acker

American experimental novelist, postmodernist writer

(her voice)

I'm a 'translator' with transgressive tendencies.
While in the process of transforming texts, I transform
myself, sometimes by going into a trance.
When that happens, I'm in transit, you could say.
The American Transcendentalists appeal to me
for that reason, the universe crossing the transom
of your mind in an energy transfer of the ages,
is how I experience it when I read them,
Emerson, Whitman, et al. I transcribe the words
that come to me as if they're not my own,
which they're not. But whose are they, I wonder?
What transpires is a transparency I didn't foresee,
the words transporting me to a place transient
as it is transactional. I am transmogrified by
a transfusion of ideas where I and other are
transposed, and I transition to a new self.
If I stay translucid, I undergo a transmigration
observable to my inner sight, yet is transphenomenal
all the same. Sci-fi writers call it transcosmic.
A transmission across time and space occurs,
is the best way to describe it, or transcribe it,
words being poor substitutes, as we know.
The suddenness of the experience is transfixing.
Though I'm not trans, I am the next gender,
strands of strangenesses notwithstanding,
entranced by the entrances and exits of time.

# Ocean Vuong

American poet

—after *Time is a Mother*

To explain the workings of his heart
was the main purpose, of what
he hardly knew, survival being
the least of it.

*

The son that brothers
the boss father
into a book
made for mother.

It's what you can make a self do
even if, especially if, it's less true
by the lie gone through,
where a made name is a jaded fame.

The dead would replace me forever,
the poet says, were I not to write
myself free of them.

The whole man has a half-life
of desire radiating from within him,
proof of who he was or is
becoming, not outlasting

the inevitable but conjoined
to it, humbly, a settlement
he can live with, or in
in the space of a poem,
albeit one being groomed
for a spontaneous brand.


*


Because he says it
does not make it true,
only less false, less
unimaginable, the way
his heart beats down a lie.

(I can now look out
of my life a little
more carelessly than
before; it's more of
the world, after all,
I belong to, he says,
no longer wide-eyed
and blinking.)

Nouns as verbs for him do the heavy lifting,
as he purples, nations, gones… his dread
at high tide turning truly dreadful, as if
doom were receiving the accolades he craved.


What hangs on his every word
if not the future he hangs onto?

The question I ask myself,
he tells us, has no answer
worth repeating
in a language
you know
cannot be translated
by anyone
but me.

# Francis Ford Coppola

American filmmaker

In the age of sequels, we're seeing
cookie-cutter film-making, says Coppola.
With gaunt cheeks and bags under
his eyes, the aging whitebeard
declares the cinematic universe
of our time 'despicable,' and
insists film should be a vehicle
of knowledge and inspiration,
of enlightenment even. But
woe betide us to keep revisiting
the same film over and over
again, it is not true cinema, that
post-apocalyptic critique of our lives
we need to see ourselves by.
He joins Scorsese* in hitting back
at the Marvel hits we're drowning in,
age of 'theme parks' without end
that unveil sameness without risk,
character's paradox left in the trash bin.
Or... is this rather the succumbing to
grumpy grand old men syndrome?


*The seeing camera violates what it sees,
says Martin Scorsese, but also revels in
the joy and glamor of the seen.

# Stanley Kubrick

American filmmaker

—after *The Shining*

In the crosshairs of his imagination
appears not horror per se, but cinematic
fear raised to the nth degree perfectly
captured by the camera-cum-vision
that no sweaty filmgoer can resist
as he or she watches in the darkened
theater we attend less and less and
more in our cranial convolutions,
the doors gushing blood
just a fraction of the human fear
he'd dance us through, with time
our partner in the screen's playback,
and central casting penetrating space
until we go over, as off a cliff, into
the Freudian murk of the father/son conflict
vast in its detailed permutations, fluid
from one expression to the next, each take
shining with amazement, psychic
experience palpably felt at eye-level,
the lens seen through tilting
our view inward and outward together
in effects zoomed in and out of—
until sealed with a real-time, technical kiss.

# Yasujiro Ozu

Japanese filmmaker

—after *Late Spring*

How we make the separations travel between
worlds, those gaps that will close no less for
the tears we shed, for, say, the daughter who
spends her years devoted to her father and,
when it comes time to marry, bows before
him in tender thanks, the entire film building
to this moment, and the floodgates open, how
they each will go their way, after he tells
the lie of his life, told in order to free her
to make her own happiness as a wife, the way
he and her mother tried, through pain, to make
theirs, and did, after years of learning, how
the father, fifty-six, persuading her his life
was ending while hers was just beginning,
so go, he says, and be rest assured, and her
husband whom we never once see on screen
is the lucky man, of course, to become the object
of such devotion, while the father in the last
scene is sitting alone in his house, peeling
an apple in one long, ribboned piece,
an ending equal to the lateness of the season
whose blossoming deep in the soil
of ordinary change, we know will go on.

# Rod Serling

American screenwriter, TV producer

He went from the WWII battlefields into the corporate
trenches of the 1950s television studio, intent on bringing
adult fare to the famously decried 'wasteland' that
broadcast all day seven days a week, but the latitude
he found there for a moral imagination gave his high-
mindedness a run for its and our money, twilit and
in the zone, writing-wise, where the real and the imagined
fused into character-driven stories of his times. Let its
holistic themes give the lie to disposable shows, and watch
sixty years on how timely the digs are he made legendary,
of the high crimes and misdemeanors we live and die by
as Americans in a hostile world, yes, of our own making.
For the channel we tune into, will be henceforth programmed
by the screen that draws us deeper and deeper into appearances
we'd do well not to lose sight of, wherever they may take us
now, re-runs of an otherworldly art, of a televised, streaming sort.

# J.D. Salinger

American writer

(his voice)

I would be untoward in my musings
were I to dwell on my self, an illusion
I have set out in my writings to disavow.
How much I owe my success in this
endeavor revolves around my understanding
of *maya*, or what we call the world.
Pleasure and pain fall away as I embrace
the non-self that is the basis of grace
as I've come to know and experience it.
Keeping intruders away has become
the imperative I live my life by, for they
only cloud my knowing, such as it is,
that I hope to purify as I grow older.
Let me alone is all I ask now, as the
question I hope the world answers.
Though in the meantime I'll have
imbued in my writings the budding
realization that if we're all Buddhas,
we're all Beelzebubs, too. Go figure.
For when the outsider on a vision quest
to see the lines blur, sees the mind
become undone, no blessing
ever after can undo the curse,
say or write what he will. Call it
his cross to carry over the long haul.

But the war one survives marks one
to the core, he for whom the bells toll,
hearing the battles sound his soul.

# The Beats

i Hell

I was at the door of Hell
one cold winter night in '88
with 'nothing' to read and
got turned away on a technicality—
the poets all lined up before me
admitted to the open reading,
while I remember Richard Hell
sitting behind his desk in the hall
of St. Mark's Church-in-the-Bowery
barring my way, staring incredulously,
a wry, quizzical look on his face,
in his hands my fresh- typed poem 'nothing.'

ii Corso

In a basement bar on Bleeker Street
Ginsberg and Yevtushenko were reading when
in a burst of wild energy Gregory Corso, in the audience,
rose to his feet and began drunkenly hurling
insults at the two distinguished poets
up on stage, the crowd sitting at their tables
startled by the interruption, the cascade
of words flowing from Corso's open mouth
almost operatic in its fury, Ginsberg trying
his best to quell his friend, offering now scolding,
now soothing words, averting yet another
scandal by say-what-you-please Bacchus.

iii Ginsberg

I wasted no time trying to score
a meeting with Allen Ginsberg
after his reading in the Village,
handing him a sheaf of my poems for
him to read. In the basement audience were
Arthur Miller and Kurt Vonnegut who
passed me walking up the stairwell
on their way out. I telephoned Ginsberg soon
after and he shouted, "I'm too busy!
And besides, I don't get paid enough!
*The New York Times* pays only $400
for an article of mine! So why
did you give me your poems?!"
"Uh…uh…It was a gift," I stuttered.
"Keep your gift!" he yelled.
(And reader, I've tried, I've tried…)
He insisted I come pick up the sheaf
of poems at his apartment located not far
from where my wife and I were living
in the East Village at the time. We climbed
the stairway to his second-story 12th St. apt.
to find the scruffy poet puttering around
an old kitchen with his young male secretary
hovering solicitously nearby. After some
awkward small talk, perhaps to make the visit
seem worthwhile, he graciously handed
me my poems, and we said our goodbyes.
We would leave for 'far-off Japan,'
as one poet has called it, soon after in '89.

# William Saroyan

American writer

—after "Going Home"

The going home Saroyan writes of happens
in stages, poignant and ambivalent, where
the young man, the narrator, tells his story
of how he landed back there by mistake,
a 'good mistake,' after two years roaming
from town to town, living in San Fran
a while, until he up and got the yen
to travel back to his beautiful hometown
in the San Joaquin Valley, in the early 1930s,
which, along with its water, is the picture
of simplicity, purity, and stillness, but also,
he adds later, of falseness, meanness, and ugliness.
The scene of the young man standing outside
his house peering in through the window
is one we're left with, until my students are
assigned to rewrite the story's ending, given
the choice of having him either reenter the old
family house in a heartwarming homecoming,
or turn around and leave it, for good.

# Pico Iyer

British-born essayist, novelist

(his voice)      —after *Autumn Light*

Write and weep.

Climbing the staircase to our 2nd floor
apartment always puts me in mind
of an approach to a shrine…

Deeply interested in the relation
to god, not in the existence of god

It's easy to come,
it drives one to distraction,
not to go for wisdom
but for its nearest approximations

Venturing to the top of my field,
I've taken refuge here in Kyoto
for rest and respite, secure
in the knowledge that what
I have here could not be had
in any other city in the world,
a city of traditional cast amid
hell-bent modernity.

# Part Five

*Gold under the sun, shining on
to wax and wane, moon-wise forward.*

# Cosmic Bandwidths

For this poet, 360-degree everyday life
consists of a panoply of submerged narratives
and relational thronging, entangled messages
and assorted mishaps, mystic copulations
and exposed incarnations all felt, heard,
and overheard on cosmic bandwidths
(as ripples in the fabric of space-time)
where heroes and villains, gods and goddesses
arise and take shape, both real and surreal via
libidinal energies. At base a peace-lover in a war-
haunted land, he depicts himself in the process
of awakening from daydreams and reimagining
the great we-all of life, those psychological landscapes
that we migrate through over time, which he
acknowledges could take place anywhere
but that happens to be, for him, in Japan,
the mysterious and ancient land of the rising sun.


*


Buddha smiling or Jesus
dialing up a newer connection
to the cosmos won't be the
final word on anything
but their own ballast
keeping us afloat in the
warm blood-soaked waters
of Mother Earth, from whom
has been fathered a death-

wish we'll never outlive, so
vast is its claim on our psyches,
History by any other name.
Sue all we will, we'll be
wheeled out from its center
like so much chafe from wheat
long out of our reach, if not sight.
Signal vibrations avail you of
the veils of appearance you'd help
restore, this talky underwear
the first of layers to come.


*


It all got so complicated, this lying
to tell the truth, but he himself
could no longer believe what he was saying,
so how could anyone else believe it?
This was the conundrum he had brought
upon himself. Grappling with it only seemed
to make things worse. For if he did voices,
then the voices, he discovered, did him.

His self's apple-babble is cycle-logical down to its roots.
In the elements of animal rumination, it has it all—
bovine vicissitudes, canine devotion, leonine splendor,
and, not least, asinine redoubtability. His serpentine
mastery speaks volumes to a religious and political
constituency he'll one day have, though not aimed for
as of yet. Sanguine he remains, and must remain, in
the face of mute incomprehension and outright hostility.
From the alpine heights to the supine depths he carries on.

*

As I read them one at a time,
her words, shiny as coins,
had weight on the page.

On the wet roads the windy rain
makes the sound of a wave
growing nearer and nearer my bed
from which I am listening
in the blackness I see.

We see him staying on top of his life,
or trying to, and we marvel at his stamina,
the soul-wearying effort required on behalf
of wholeness he rallies us all around.
We pass with him through those orbits, not
unnoticed by him, but ever-circling, staying
close by and wondering at our shared space,
procession-like proceeding as if skin-on-skin,
arm in arm, hand in hand him and us we go.

What we hear, or overhear him saying is:
Spare me the fantasy, please, of helping others,
or of satisfying their needs
and yes
I posted some pretty
outlandish things recently.

*

He's doing things you would
not dream of doing.

Alan. Be still.
Now you are touching on
mysteries I cannot fathom.
Channeling spirits is a time-
honored tradition among poets
reaching back to Merrill and Yeats
and of course, much further.
I cannot presume to understand it.

One thing is sure: it offers new views
of our place in the universeCity…

Botsford has a loyal kinship with the stars.
He forges ahead on a rocketship that roars
into a space that's outta here he calls inner.
What shambles he makes of poor earth
we'll not wait to find out. Time for the face
of things to put in an appearance, a birth
we can ill-afford not to enable the sinner
in our midst who, we now hear, rejoices
in plenitude not of accolades but of voices
tuned to perfection he plumbs, called depth,
yet where it'll lead we dare not concede:
he's a piper of music the blind can read.

He's such a loving guy
I can see his sky
from halfway round the world.
But he puts his plan on hold
until he can say why
falling down the rabbit-hole
of history is, at heart, no lie
that isn't in the end unfurled
from deep within the dreaming eye.

# Tourist in Engakuji Temple

—foreign tourist  (his voice)

He sits on the bench eyeing
us passersby. Where is he from,
I wonder? I'll detach myself
from the group—I've been
with them all morning—and
meander over to a bench of
my own. Mine has sunlight
beating down on it, while his
is perched in the shade. Either
way, I can keep him in my
field of vision while we sit
here, each of us perhaps wondering
about the other. After all, I'm
half his age, it would appear, what
with his white hair and unshaven
face. When I passed by in front of
him did he notice, I wonder, that
we're both tall and slim? Did he
appreciate my aqualine features
mirroring his own, with short-cropped
hair framing our white skin? I felt
his gaze, at any rate, which infused
a charge between us momentarily.
The birds are making a racket in
the temple. He seems not to mind,
though, maybe even enjoying
them fluttering about in the shadowy

eaves, while the ground basks in
the sunlight. The gnarled ancient
trees in front of us make strange
companions, taking one's mind off
the people swarming around them.
Theirs is a massive but gentle
presence, offering those like us
a spot of comfort, re-energizing us
before we have to get up off our
benches and make our way back
into the crowds this Saturday
morning in Kita-Kamakura, far
from Tokyo, far from the upcoming
U.S. election, far from the world
that is changing, even as we speak.

# Expatriate Writer

—American writer in Japan  (his voice)


i


You're a good guy, Alan, and
what I wouldn't give to know more
about your exilic life in Japan where
we've all dug in our heels with the cruel
passing of the years. Who knows better
than we do the sound of the stranger's footfalls
echoing in foreign stairwells
which we climb up and down day after day
to meet our inglorious fate, now
colored over with pastel truths
once bold, once deep in the pulsing world.
Where has it gone now, I ask the bone.


ii


Alan, we writers skirmish in the no man's land
where readers do or don't read what we've written,
but press on we must, into full-fledged battle!
Not to stretch the metaphor here, given the world
we're living in, but still, war is an apt metaphor for
all our lives, whether it's just beginning or near its end,
for fight we must, for a piece of land we can call
our own, the place we take our stand in, to give
what is ours to give. Everything else is just fake
news, don't you think? Truth-seekers, unite!

# Jeffrey Angles

—American & Japanese poet, translator (his voice)


i


Alan's nuts, but I won't bolt. Stupendous poets
I'm surrounded by, what's one more give or take
on my pendulum? He swings, or I can, not back
and forth but up and down, mood-wise. Careful
my steps must be. His shoes aren't ones I'd walk
in, in a thousand years, though far he's come
in them. What we say to each other in our journey
of conversations, is, I admit, of little interest,
though to be cajoled out of what I'm pigeonholed
in, would be cause for gratitude. He's even less
enamored of labels than I, which makes sense,
certainly, for a reluctant Japanophile he won't
claim he is. And do I care? I wear my label
proudly despite the wear and tear of it in my ears.
What ho! The Brits say? Ah so, say the Japs.
So what? add the Yanks. So the sum of it is…?
Someday your Prince Charming will come,
though not the way it sounds. We do rounds
of shots, and come up for air thinking and
drinking, taking drafts in gulp-size umphs!
The Donald Trumps of the world are on the rise,
where will that leave us, a perished thought?
Alan has taught us a thing or two after all.
Alan in having no fear, is fear itself. Hence my tear.
Alan's nuts, yes, but I won't bolt. He's batty

but in his belfry are lightning bolts
bottled up, which he makes boldly felt as
broken cadences, brocaded circumstance.


ii


Alan, it's a world we inhabit
that, like it or not, inhabits us.
That's why my money's on self-
possession, since our time on earth's
limited, and the self we owe our lives to
needs space and time to be defined.
Otherness be damned? Not
exactly. They with free-agency
come and go as they please, but human
interaction being what it is, team-
work's needed all the way down the
line—of sight if not of vision—from
cradle to grave. Why else be a
language-speaker, right? Left-over
honey gets stored away for another
day—that's a commonwealth I can
believe in, if not pledge myself to,
the source of everything human I
won't despise, but allows me to
realize myself en route to an ever
larger Self challenging me up ahead.
People do that for each other as you've
done for me today, for which I thank
you, kind sir. We made a road map to
nowhere I've been before, that I found
myself tripping over my words to get to,
just to see what would come next! A

revelation, if you must know. You have
a fearlessness, sir, I've seldom known,
about the unknown and all that, in which
we now both have a stake as of today.
Human ties, it's been called. It's a pleasure
and privilege to know (and unknow) myself
in the process. Ties do that, moving us
along new tracks to new places which
gratitude keeps opened and my heart
bows to. A good day we've made
a new memory of, which for now I'll
cherish. This I call the ground beneath
my feet which a poem can never provide.
To be true to it is what writing asks,
but seldom delivers. This my life knows
and now unknows too, the venerable
whitehead you've been for me today
notwithstanding. An understanding
achieved bi-laterally is, in my book,
what being alive's about. Love rarely
enters the picture, mind you, except
for what we call the 'bigger' picture,
when as Dante says it moves the stars
moon and sun in the heavens to picture-
perfect synchronicity. That City—
cosmic you call it—is off-limits to all
save, yes, Poets, their visions needed
for the machinery we rely on to keep
everything aligned. May it continue being
so with us, neither one of us a chess piece for
the other. Let us be + come + whatever
+ we + wheel! Sealed by a 'kiss' I hope
is not amiss, since for me there's no
better path to discovery.

iii

Alan hits a wall for every ball
we catch and don't throw back,
and won't he get frustrated by
it all?! The surprise awaiting him
is no fall from grace but from
the case-by-case that keeps
the ball rolling, and for good
reason, too. So all hail the good
thief of our hearts, that we heart
back and forth, back and forth…
east to west, south to north…
Let the world spin in our heads
and the zeitgeist go where it will!

He is the tree the dog pees on
He is the tree lightning hits
He is the tree leaves grow from
He is the tree roots hide under
He is the tree the sky loves
He is the tree that grows far
into the world to tell its story
that others climb to see what
they would see he is the tree
that rhymes with free, and whose
rings round and round sing
of the soft and hard ground
He is the tree whose fruit, when
low hanging, is stolen for loot
He is the tree birds build nests in
He is the tree that deep into
the future has already grown past

Come on baby baby hold me tight
We got a free-wheeling delight
He won't whimper when he bangs
out a letter as god is our witness
He's smokin' in a time capsule
he sends us through space
What a gorgeous energy but
can he keep up the pace?
Holy is his matrimony
to his beloved wife,
and holy is his strife—
we'll ease him into the next round
where the lost everyday are found
on the way of the island.
Knock knock he keeps coming
Knock knock he won't be going
Knock knock he's a gorgeous man
to behold
He takes us back to where back
is front and time heals all our
unhealed wounds, to where
the unsaid things finally get said
and unborn are the dead.
Such a catch his imagination is,
that stretches the universe wide open
and foolishly, beautifully deep.


For the poet
the instrument is
the whole body
of sound mind.

To say it whole
he gave everything away
and finally could get down
to writing what only he had to say
—that day in court won after
a long dark night of the soul.

He stumbles into
lines left write
and center.
They tighten like twine
into tales only he could tell
sample the seams
of his dreamed-up lines
and you'll find they unravel
at the merest touch—
into one's hands falls
unspooled yarn in a tangle
of verbs and nouns.
Where had his story gone,
if he had ever had one?

iv

Alan shakes us up but won't spit
us out, he's galling to some, beguiling
to others. We drink up a storm and
have some fun at nobody's expense,
what it costs us is a walk in the sun.
He smiles and we raise our glass to the man
with his foot in leaves of grass, a walk
he takes with us for a future we can, yes,
believe in. He's supportive where we once
were dismissive. Can we help it if we

read the territory he treads backward
to front, only to be lost in the entrails
of another world, another galaxy?

Alan likes the look of things in love with
the depths of things, and where the twain
meet is his muse of fire and fusion. Who can
keep up with a man like him, is the question
nobody has the answer to. It's step by step
to the places unknown as they are unforgiving.
Try all we will, should he get lost in the night,
who will go looking for him? With whose
light can we follow him and bring him out
again, is the worry we all have. Yet smile
we will, for the good fortune he bestows,
a boon not only of nature but of time and
space we know next to nothing about,
a handsome if lonely fate on our pickled
shores. How he dances on those shells
to restore the sound of the ocean within
their whorls, is a miracle we witness,
though who would believe it in our day?
He aspires to the moment we can share,
a heart-breaking pittance where art is
concerned. His is a forrest gump of a
portrait offered to the mirrors of us,
and who can say whether he jumps
the moon for his next poem, and when
will he land back on earth and all the
horrors she harbors? Wait we will, for
whatever the lumpen proles among us
can unearth—and lovingly give birth to.

*

Alan, as handsome as he is,
doesn't play by the rules
and he knows it, we know it,
everyone knows it and they
in disbelief or in envy look
on half-wishing for the other
shoe to drop so they can
say, Hey, he stands on sand
after all. Or, hey, his feet
are made of clay. But it's
here we all meet on common
ground, he reminds us, and
for that we won't forgive him.
The foot you shoot is your
own, we insist, even though
we know better. His foot is
legion! His footwork on
display in the Land of Roots
is astounding, as we can see.

His is the nutrient of many minds.
Allowing for the build-up of
a cacophony of voices.

Who will follow him in
his journey?

He's not looking for followers,
he's looking for inspiration.

Fact is, Americans will knock
the inspiration out of him.

A wrap-around wall of
sound imbibing the mysteries.

# Expatriate Poet

—American poet in Japan (his voice)

i

Hail fellow well met—
the diet of Japanese can get
lonesome and, lest we forget,
inverted so that dry turns wet
and sticky, like natto we eat
with white rice on a table set
for the family to whom I owe a debt
of gratitude, and don't I know it!
To be repaid in daily rounds that let
me show love and affection quiet
as the temple I enter on shoeless feet
to pray our lives continue to abut
the sacred and profane in a duet
no saint would pray for, nor sinner repeat.

ii

Alan, we part waves, you and I, on an ocean
I didn't see coming, and for that you have
my thanks, a twist in the tale you tell, full
of wonder and armed with love and depth
to be savored slowly, I hope, as we swim
these waters together, what I've a longing
to do with a mate in lonely climes, your
rhymes keeping me company, gently, for

a fellowship that Melville pointed us all
towards, I believe, after reading your take.
In the wake of him and others is an epic
you've succeeded in making, sanguine, starlit
for the long nights ahead, and true to soul.

# The Classroom

i

When it's that time of business
to close the door and make eye contact
and move more and more toward
a center we all can gather in,
settle in, communicate in, is the time
to let words fly with wings we give them,
and they give us, to meet in a fluent, consummate sky.

*

In the book of words whose pages are numbered
I feel the time pass me so quickly
that I run out of space musically.

ii  Rayna (her voice)

You are kind, and I don't mind
you looking at me. You're easy on
the eye yourself. Well, here we are
and the path gets narrower where
the two of us close in on it. What
brings us near will take us far,
past the worries over the darkness
ahead, and the anxieties about limits
we need to heed, and our desires
we no longer have to be afraid of.
Because you and I both know this won't

work if the loveless in us gains
where love would put down roots.
The quarrel we've been having in slow
motion for so long won't blossom, now
that we have our sights set on bigger
things. We have the world to love,
and we each will show patiently how,
like a secret pact lovers share at night,
in our dreams each of us lives the Other.


iv  Noa (her voice)


Prof, we didn't know who you were before,
and still don't, but we'll answer your
questions and follow the lesson you've planned.
Mistakes were made and now we'll unmake them,
though you're bound and tied by our rules now.
What's in store we know only too well,
but we won't tell. Welcome to hell.
Pray to your god all you will, not until
Hell freezes over will things change here.
This is how things have been done and
will always be done, so help you and your
magic sandcastles made on paper that won't
make a bit of difference here, no matter
where we sit. Close our eyes and open our books
is all that you'll get from us—says our chorus.
You won't get us with yesterday's poems.
There are a dozen ways and reasons why Rome
wasn't built in a day, and we're staying that way,
the holy noises you make notwithstanding.
There's no pushing us or pulling us,
we've got nowhere to go, don't you see?

It's called Law, and its sheriff is History,
not harmony. Testing the waters, you are,
it's clear to see, but you'll drown before
you find the key that unlocks our common ancestry.
Witness what you want, but stars we are not.
Heaven to us is tied up tight as a knot:
ages spent by sages who went to their graves
one by one wondering how to climb the rope
—all you've got to get you there, is hope.
Don't waste your time climbing, for every
mistake will cost you your direction.
If I were you, I'd be careful from now on.


v.  Haruna (her voice)


We're a 'group of good girls' with no ulterior designs.
We've got to learn and you're our prof.
How we go about it is for you to decide,
but we'll always choose the right side
even though many of us are left-handed.
Teach us, then, to laugh and learn and
grow as a group, we'll get there when
we get there. For now, see you next week
when together, we all of us, will begin again.


vi  Seiya (her voice)


There's my prof. He'll see me but
won't feel me feeling his vibe.
If I stay still long enough, who will
he be, wandering eye he seems to have?
I'll keep mine in my head, and watch
what he does… just as I thought!

He passed by and in his breeze
I had him on his knees, the puppy.
I'm young and available, & he knows it too.
What expectations I'll foment for
the great revolution he envisions
in our house, the one whose back door
he'll see a lot of in upcoming days.
We wish him well, and will work
hard with him, as he advised. But
old his age, a cage he can't come
out of, in public, anyway. Still,
I like what he sees in me, and
will not horde my energies when
in this field he calls our togetherness.

vii

Dwelling in fire, you're a
salamander of night
peering through the flames
at the day you'd ignite.
Here, you say, is where love
assumes its contours and
draws spirit close into
the heat-swelled heart
of time.

# Takahiro

—Japanese university student (his voice)

Mr. Botsford knows his way around us
better than before. He's been through
the rocky gorge and seen the silvery
moon high in the sky above the cliff's
rim, and learned the constellations'
names one starry pool at a time. He
foots the bill on our territory, though,
which must gall him, however star-
crossed he remains. How much longer
we'd like to know but dare not ask.
He ventures deep into our silent realms
and lets our echo echo his wants and
needs, open as a flower in spring. I
hear his song better than I did before.
What calling he lives by I can only
guess at, though. Peace he drums up
when our tribe gathers is a boon I
won't belittle. Big the guns are that stay
pointed between his eyes, I fear, which
perhaps explains his shy confidence
landing so near the core of our Japan
he says he'll never know. True, dat.
The will he musters for the try, makes
me weep silently within. In outbound
lanes he would travel, but there his
story begins to unravel. For once the
deed's done, aren't we done for?

And once the word's spoken, aren't
we its token? It's a fear legitimate
by any measure save his, poor guy,
poetic though he waxes. Doesn't he
know the mysteries he calls to, will
wane just as surely as nightly moon?

# Harajuku Café

- Japanese female café patron (her voice)

The honey over your shoulder has
eyes for me but I'll ignore him.
I know he's listening intently to our talk.
Too bad he can't get an eyeful of my rack!
He'll just have to suffer my indifference
as we carry on with our gossip,
let him eavesdrop all he wants.
The window seat he's got gives him
honeypots galore passing by.
I don't see him resisting his
    roving eye.
What a threesome we could make
were he more of a beefcake.
But those clothes and that haircut's
on the cheesy side, while all ears
he remains. Too bad you can't swing
round for a gaze of him yourself.
He's in my line of sight as I watch
him read and write… But, well, it's high
time we left. It's been tight!

# Mermaid

Japanese translator (her voice)

Everybody's fishing for
what they can't see
beneath the surface of waters
they cannot reach
past the depths they
will never plumb
except by the echo of my voice
you're hearing as I speak.
We take pleasure in giving
the measure to our wants
in words we rightfully treasure
but it's silence I wrap
myself in, for you to peel
away, layer by layer, were we
sitting together by a watery pool
whispering and lightly splashing
droplets upon each other's
bared skin… Sssshhhhhh,
I won't tell if you won't
who I would want you to be…
Anyway, you see right through
me, and I see you for what you are,
for now, hard by the body of my softness,
and that's good enough for me.

# Expatriate Poet

—Australian poet in Japan (his voice)

Alan, I had you pegged wrong.
What shields you from a song
as vulnerable as yours must
take a hide as rhino-thick
as they come. Good lord, son,
the crash-landing your flights
of fancy have avoided all these
years is nothing short of
a miracle, but a miracle
is what you sound like, milk
or no milk, to these jaded
ears of mine. The blade I've
got buried deep in the polis cuts
a bargain hard and cold
as the steel our lives are
made of. There's no other way
to survive this world, as god
is my witness. How alive your
words sound in spite of the
rounds of death and destruction
our English lingo has wrought
on the world is testimony, I
concede, to the power of human
revival—spiritual and all that.
But who has time to rhyme
with nature anymore except our
Aboriginal folk who, as any

Aussie will tell you, got the
short end of the stick of history
which rules the land, the seas
and the skies in my neck of
the neighborhood. It's called
global—and from where I sit
it's most if not all of the pie no
poet's finger will even get near.
The rough and tumble out here—
for all the waste and blood and
pain—trumps the peaceable kingdom
you call inside but which I'll
call—excuse me—nowhere.
It's a hole in the wall
your wholeness opens
through which I can see,
it's true, a whole new
world we'll never visit
in any of our lifetimes.

But still, the chink in the wall
serves as a reminder: he
connects here to there,
the visible to the invisible,
so we can recall the balance
so easily lost in our world today.
It's a shame the shaman isn't
better known. Either way, we own
the terms he would set up
as the future's. It's a set-up
no matter which way he turns.

# Dr. Yanagawa

—Japanese general doctor (his voice)

The trail of blood the *gaijin*
leave wherever they go, hardens
into the House of Hate that this
one here must inhabit he calls
"School," schooled in the ways of
us Japanese whose days are ancient
as they are Newtonian. Yes, mastery
of nature, if not of English, has taught
me a thing or two about the West. Heed
the caution you would throw to the winds
or the House will crumble under the weight
of gravity you know little about—history
by any other name. Who, sir, are you to speak
of the future when the past clouds our view
of it, like a fog that never lifts. Nippon
has its mysteries, to be sure, but he
from foreign shores can never wade
into its waters without tides and cross-
currents endangering his every step.
Remember: the sea you see is not
the sea we see. Icy cold, too, to the
touch for both of us, though we
Japanese have warmed to you Yanks
over the years. Hawaii alohas me
and my family, but it's mostly for money,
I know. You've brought your privilege
into my land and expect a glad-hand

to last a lifetime? Don't count on it.
Madder than a hatter are you if you do.
We sell-outs have a job to do, the point
gotten to, keeping us on course, whatever
wide-angle lens you may see through.
The film unrolls for the parts we play—
me the doctor, you the patient, though
believe me my patience is more than tried
by my talking to you. Seize the day!,
you Yanks say. But for we Japanese,
it's Take it to the bank, or tank! Ha-ha-ha!
The plank you walk on, on a pirate's dime,
means we're now out of time. Bye-bye.

# Hospital Nurse

— hospital counter nurse, Kamakura (her voice)

The tall, white-haired gaijin-san lights
up our space with his eyes. I'll steal a glance
at him when he looks away. It's small
in the distance I am, but I can feel
when his glancing eyes land on me. A thrill,
I admit, but he's married. There's his wife
and his son, tall like he is. I wonder where
he's from? Who says we Japanese girls
can't have fun on the job? Here where people
come to die, or get better, or get born, even,
there's no other place I'd rather work.

# Immigration Officer

— Immigration Office counter, Yokohama (her voice)

There the tall *gaijin* hails us
in the gentle parade he and his wife
have made, the two of them now sitting,
chatting together like friends, or
lovers even, were the white hair
he wears regally a sign of the
sheerness of her purity's veil.
She's the stronger of the pair,
that's clear. And by his eyes
he knows it, too, the redeemed
and the true, that the two of
them, holding firm by their
star, are.

# Dr. Kobayashi

—Japanese psychiatrist, Kamakura (his voice)

i

Alan-san has a willing smile
and a peaceful demeanor to go
with it, and where he goes, his wife
goes with him. A beautiful couple
to these doctoring eyes, and I've
seen plenty. Where he goes in
the months and years ahead I hope
I'll be there also, for something
about him is a prize. Too early yet
to tell. He's shy, which is no surprise,
being barely toilet-trained in our
language. And our land buffets
him around like the milkweed seed
he is, the four winds having a field
day with him, I hear. Caution is
advised, for I am here to see
that he survives and, tossing
his demons aside, thrives.

ii

Alan-san aligns himself with
a fate he can't control—who can?—
and admits pain when it comes
calling. But he has the wherewithal

of his imagination, which carries
one such as him far into the unknown,
which he makes his dwelling-place,
a tiresome challenge for most
but for him a necessity, a pot
at rainbow's end goading him on
under its iridescent bands of colors,
were it visible on the road he's on,
'Open' he calls it, to his dying day.


iii  the receptionist (her voice)


He announces his aura
by voice, and it's a cool
million he floats on, a
tithe he ties himself to us
by, to which I growl my
approval, or purr, given
half a chance in our dance.
He weathers the storms I've
heard tell about, and we seed
the clouds for the rain to wash
his pain away, medicinally of course.
The mind he must have to find
his way by, must be on cyclical
mode, try all he will to get anywhere
new in our land, whose default setting,
he should understand, is return, return,
lest the future turn up non-Japanese
and out of our hands.

iv

Alan-san brings the heft of his wife
and what's left of his life to bear
on the moment he lives fully and
humbly, his wherewithal a wisdom
he would embrace in the face of
the odds against him, even as he
watches events unfold from a perch
affording him a view of the ages
that few would believe, a love
grounded in the reality of his
imagination, it would seem, above
and beyond the otherworldly bliss
we associate it with, for the imaginary
lifts each of us into the future where
spirit commingles with flesh and redeems
it whole, what some might call soul.

v

Alan-san chooses wellness over wealth,
holds no rancor for the wounds borne,
and values his marriage as the refuge
it is, from the trials of his job teaching
college students that use his wits
only up to a point, beyond which by
nature and temperament he will not go.
He floats through his workdays bobbing
in the waters of incomprehension, his voice
unheard, his thoughts unarticulated, as he tries
to blend in, not wanting to be seen
as he now thinks to himself:

Our rebellion spirit, once a fountain of possibility,
has it gone the way of corporate dominion?
The commercial 'you' has taken over
the private 'I', determining God's,
absent a last-minute appearance,
evolving emptiness at the heart
of the world, pierced as we are by
knowledge of our meaninglessness,
poetry's will to significance notwithstanding.
Wherefore woman's revelation, or is it
revolution? We aspire to hold on to change
wherever we find it, only for it to outpace
us in the quotidian mess of our lives.

# The Circus Lion Freed

— after 'Will,' Rancho dos Gnomos Santuário, Brazil, 2006

I died and went to heaven, or thought I did
when after thirteen years in a circus cage
I got set free in a sanctuary, the grass
under my feet for the first time, and logs
to claw as I pleased, and the ground soft
enough to roll around on, and the sky
bluer than the water I can swim in any
time I want. It's my kind of heaven
and if the god of lions is listening,
whatever else is in store for me let me
find out on my own four legs freely,
no more in want, no more in ache,
but here in the savannah of my dreams.

# Part Six

*He lowers the bar
for higher learning.
Everyone gets in on
the pitch to the stars.*

# George Clooney

American actor

—after *Gravity*, dir. Alfonso Cuardon

Man *in vitro* waiting for time
to give him space to breathe, sees
an opening and seizes it, a race
not to the finish but to the beginning
of life, earlier than lately it's been.
His brick-and-mortar self meets
resistance from his straw man,
an edifice unto itself, wherever the
flow ends up taking them both.
Meanwhile the orbit he's in has
its own gravity pulling him back
down to earth, to plant his feet on.
The vehicle he's in houses all his
hopes for the future, a place space
is hurtling toward him as he, imagining
it now, meets it halfway like a hand
that, reaching out, seeks to be held
or that seeks to hold fast to somewhere,
or someone, in this moment tethered to all
the amplitude he'll ever need.

# William Wordsworth & Samuel Coleridge

English Romantic poets

—after *Pandaemonium,* dir. Julien Temple

Dorothy wishes Samuel were one
with her, but William knows better
and would insist on Poetry's project
as the Revolution, in embryo, it's always
been, a potential of the New to outstrip
the Old, the woods and glades fodder
for the books to come, a greatness equal
to the Nature giving it birth, in time.
Sarah bears the burdens of domestic
bliss, while the two poets drink tea
and compose lyrical ballads for
future fame, tying their fortunes to
eternity's feathered strokes across
the inked page, each line
for the ages, his, opium penned.

# Samuel Coleridge's *Mariner*

His cup runneth over abounding in inspiration
for which, guilt-driven, he had to pay lifelong
a certain penance, each poem a confession
varying from distempered talk to high song,
emotion not recollected tranquilly but powerful
feelings in spontaneous overflow, the Angel
of Reckoning through prophecy distilled
his life of poetry a curse and death fulfilled.

# John Keats

English Romantic poet

He welled up and willed himself
to be a poet, and would die apace
with the sweat running down his face.
Severn was with him to the end,
drawing his portrait at his bedside,
as letters from Fanny went unread.
Writ in water he said he was, and
meant it, watching himself seep away.
They came and burned the furniture,
his room stripped bare, nothing left
but his poetry, melancholic, lines to die for.

# Mary Shelley

English novelist

—after *Frankenstein*

You concocted out of chaos a birth
perpetually stillborn, yet fertilized
by an imagination Romantic and radical,
post-French revolution, a labor of
wit, despair, revenge, and prophecy.
What freedom denied looks like,
monsterish in its slave's guise,
you took to heart, and raised in words
the failure of the body (politic) to create.
How loving and fragile the call
of the creator's mate, abandoned
in the end to his piecemeal fate,
heir of modernity, a cursed blood-line
of an experiment gone wrong,
song of yourself, song of all of us.

# Charles Dickens

English novelist

—after *A Christmas Carol*

The soul of Scrooge, withered
and cramped, forgot the spirit
of Christmas, or had buried it
beneath his hoarding miserliness
from years of money-making
and money-worshipping. Love
did not stand a chance in his
life, so entombed, so emotionally
stunted and crimped he was,
that it did not stand a chance.

*

It's tragically true that banks own this world.
For Scrooge, money is huge.
For Tiny Tim, money is slim.

How do you sleep, bankers?

Money transmuting in all its guises
falls to common ground and rises
like baked dough.

Come, thief, go take what you like.

Plunge your money
into the capital
of Love.


Too much mind-bending
and spirit-sending
beats moneylending
any time.

# Thomas Hardy

English novelist, poet

He traversed the city from country by-ways
he left behind then returned to late in life,
there to write his cherished verse and pine
for what he'd lost, a world gone too soon
save for in memory's pastures where he'd
graze to his heart's content and mind
the lives of others far away in time.

# Walt Whitman & Emily Dickinson

American poets

I have made the compiling of *Leaves*
my main life's work, Whitman announced
in so many words early on. And so it was,
year after year new poems were added, until
the original 12 poems grew to
400 in the death-bed edition.

Did Walt Whitman sell us an idea
of what America could be, or did he live it?
Whitman's conflict of producing within
these tensions actually fed his creativity.
In the end, he is the experience of
America in whom his story culminates.

The good words are good
to hear, would they be spoken
in time. But late or early,
space is the place for them, says
the spider in its web,
filament after filament
launched forth, tenuous,
fragile, yet patiently spinning
each new thread
out of the invisible
again and again, into
the visible world.

*

In most if not all cultures ceremonies and rules—
whether political, social, or religious—enforce patriarchy.
Politicians are the masters of round-the-clock ceremonies.
Science, on the other hand, is based on experiment,
a matriarchal impulse? to see
where the unknown takes you.

With Emerson left in charge of the whole history
of American lit, practically speaking,
Whitman, America's no holds bard,
intertwines both streams or impulses
in his poetry—a song of myself both as niche
(ceremony) and as destination (the unknown)…

Perfectly beautiful and wise, for me,
are the lines of Whitman at his best
(moonlighting wasn't long for him;
he made sunlight speak
in an idiom all its own).

My divine is both
inside and out, Whitman says essentially.
*Leaves of Grass* was the gift
the Divine Imagination gave him,
that he would pass on to all those
in need of or in joy of reading it
(which, by his lights, was every single American!).

Not to read "Song of Myself" in sequence
but to dip into it at whim here and there allows

one the distinct pleasure of reading a random line
or set of lines of which the poem is so brilliantly composed.

And there is no archetype, the poet reminds us,
that doesn't already run through you to carry you along.

(The energetic flow
his poetry embodies
belies the stone tomb
he had built to bury
his bones for eternity.)

*

For my money, though,
Dickinson drills down
deeper into the core of Being.

While conjuring
in the language of night
lines breathless before noon,
Emily stamped her style
upon the ground
of her being,
and became her style.

At the top of her game
nearly every day of her life.

*

What do you do if you reject the terms
your society has imposed on you

and you're a woman in mid-19th century
America named Emily Dickinson?
They refuse to be a wife, for one,
(Emily Dickinson was 'they' before
they used 'they' in the 21st century.)
remaining unmarried their whole life.
They refuse to bear children, mothering
instead, their own mother when she falls ill
and creating their offspring they call poems.
Their object of romantic interest
may be of the same sex, in the guise
of their sister-in-law, their muse
and possible lover. And their days
are spent at home in their father's house,
days and nights filled with writing poetry,
unconventional poetry at that, replete
with capitalized nouns and runaway
dots and dashes, certain to marginalize
them further. (The word tedium could not be
further from their lexicon, let alone their experience.
They reveled in the details of domestic life
like few poets before or since, even as they
rebelled against the constraints of female
domesticity.) But more to the point,
they reject the terms society would impose
on them by assiduously redefining those terms
in ways more congenial to their nature,
which Emily defiantly does—their feathered
hope, their invented or pierless faith, their
fickle fame, their tragic glory, their hinged noon
all are ways for them to confront this discrepancy
between who they were and who society
would allow them to be, a gap whose enormity

would charge their poems with an all-
consuming wonder and opposition
honed by a sublime poetic technique
in the service of states, spiritual and psychical,
that cannot here be summarily pinned
down or known, the dictionary of their life
and work self-made, a garden tended to,
(Love knows no outside)
clearing a space for the flowers and plants to grow.
(Dickinson, an explorer of the natural world and
of psychic space, is a cosmic dreamer of shifting personas.
The poetry explodes into details discerning
as they are enigmatic, elusive, ungraspable.)
They didn't want to be unheard.
Unseen, perhaps, but not unheard.
(You may think they wanted applause,
or a dallop of praise, but they'd sooner
watch the moon in its phases
circling the nondescript sky night after night
than bask in the heat of the sun
burning their short-lived days away.)

In sum, resistance to circumstance was in their instance
affirmation of their real existence,
to their soul's admittance but few,
without the assistance of publication
but with singular persistence
wedded to Circumference, their true business.


*


Whitman's seashore,
Thoreau's pond,

Dickinson's house—
all patterned after before.

Pattering of patterning
or patterning the pattering,
nothing's pat when everything's apt
to be rapt, no pent-up serpent,
libido not at liberty
to disclose what it knows
ego censures for the sake
of closure, not erasure,
the one step forward, two steps
backward chance
to suffice for now,
and for when then comes
calling in opened stance.

Twoness blanks the violence of one,
mirror given in nearness outgrowing,
as you stand before it looking
at what's after.

# Virginia Woolf

English novelist

She lived under a cascade of words
she eventually drowned in, hearing
birds speaking in Greek to her while
writing her way to shore. But the river
of words reclaimed her by a sea
of voices that ended up inside her head,
no way out but through sentence by
sentence, a gushing stream of consciousness
that landed her in history, a voice
on a wave of time.

# Dylan Thomas

Welsh poet

(his voice)

I tolled the bell of my tongue
and the steeple of the air chimed
with my name. Hip hip the poet!
With a booming deathless voice
I caroled the winter ghosts to please
the shadows in me, coral sea deep
past shores I now recall in *his* sleep.

# Les Murray

Australian poet

(his voice)

The fury of this, the angel of that
duel over the roundness of flat
earth back in the day when night
told the story of aboriginal light.

# Seamus Heaney

Irish poet

(his voice)

It feels fantastic fighting
into the light through
the darkness-sway.
I fought my whole life
to earn my death
triumphantly,
fearless to the end.
Of the kind I was
to bind the wounds
along the way
and have my say
you'd hardly recognize
were you not a poet too.
Them's true words
we'd embrace
for the lies we'd erase,
field-work hewn to
over high roads and low.
It's the friend, not foe,
I'd retrace my footsteps for.

# Angela Carter (in Japan)

English writer

(her voice)

She, who is me, wore a kimono
for the sake of costume play, theater
he indulged for the two of us. Show
me who you are, he said, and I'd teeter
on the brink of everything I knew
to be real, until I fell, arms akimbo,
into a puppet-like grace. I love you,
he'd say, laughing, to please her.

# Kanishk Tharoor

Indian writer

(his voice)

The swashbuckling narratives of self
conceived by modernity is not my cup
of tea. I prefer a staider, compartmentalized
fixture of self, multicultural to be sure, and
easily displaced onto newer terrain in a
cosmopolitan way, but still constructed
by history, built to last.

# Chinua Achebe

Nigerian novelist   i.m.

The power of his voice accrues
to its proverbial wisdom, uttered
with both humility and pride,
sincerity and irony. This is
a writer whose African heritage,
its pre-colonial histories, finds
equal footing with its colonial
realities and post-colonial liberations.
He knew that things fall apart
but that they also come together
again by the thinnest of threads,
in his case via a literary imagination
that gave Africa back to Africans
and opened the eyes, ears and minds
of an Anglo readership to how Africans
view themselves and their culture,
in the language, however, of the former
colonizers. We have him to thank
for uncovering African stories for
the modern era, for future writers
who would follow in his footsteps
that lead down a dead man's path.

# Margaret Wertheim

Australian writer

(her voice)

Fires the feminine ignites into brainstorms
stemmed in the night, spread in the darkness
for a fight I'd take to anyone who'd disown
the woman on the throne. We have burned
our way here, read: earned our way here,
and here is where we aim to stay, graceful
as the mist. What women want is this face
to ward off the evils that would bury them
in the ground of being, never becoming
what they're meant to be. That is how I see
the worlds coming round and past me
in plentiful orbits, elliptically. The genius
among us foretells, ingeniously, what we
cannot see coming, and for that I'll be there,
ready and waiting, words heated from below
like a lava flow pitching forward its slow
steady stream that remakes the ground it covers.

# Lykke Li

Swedish pop star

(her voice)  —after a YouTube concert video 2011, NYC

The songs my music presents are all wrong
for the doe-eyed Disney crowd, but
I keep packing 'em in between my legs.
I've got it and I'll keep it, that's my story
The price I've paid drives me madder every day
but who am I to say it's not "fun"?
Boys don't interest me, it's men I eat up
I choose 'em like my instruments in a shop
We either connect or not
Hey, it's a dirty business but I'm no mess
I know just what I'm doing, don't think I don't
The slumming I do on tour is slutty, I admit
But don't think it's any better for guys.
We gals know the deal— we play to feel
found not lost, and to keep it real
'cuz everything else everyone can steal
—your heart, your time, your money, your trust,
your art even— call it the music career from hell.
But, well, it's my bratty attitude that's got me
this far, brainy beauty though I may be.
I won't slam how things are in the U.S. of A.
whether it's going down the tubes or not.
Here I'm loved and here I'll gladly stay
as long as they pay me and pay me well.
Impeccable are my qualifications, after all.

I'll come back here with my wanderlust & attention
at the blink of an eye, descending further in the luck we call
home. ...Oh, another interruption, is there no rest?
Despite all this running around, I feel blessed
Hand-groping hips I'll swivel and grind
Don't you Americans know I'm an unholy find?
The trials I've gone through for this taunting smile
I've earned like any glam-star before me—
in shit-housed open mics that left me shaking & nauseous.
But this is what I've always wanted
and by this I remain haunted.
If (sublimated) desire's what I trade on, it's always
the ghost I dub "Chance" that has
the last word and so, you said it, the last dance!

# Wendy C. Oritz

American writer


(her voice) —after an interview, 2016

I've spit out my story
with all its gory details
to have my say heard
a grrrl's way, but won't
be fucked again is my
policy, no matter what
gets said. It's a cold
day in hell where we
women writers get laid
for the almighty buck.
You heard it here first.
A token reminder of
battles to come, and
I don't pun for fun.
She-all is the wheel
I've spun, no hee-haw
in this battle zone.
You know the drill:
agency is what I kill
for, music to die for
already in your ears,
though a zine I'll
open to, legs and all.
Lonely woman I'm not,
we hanging together

like this is all the bliss
I need, ass-wipes won't
figure in my calculations,
not now, not ever. This
grrrl's nature is bi-.
A wonderful life George
never knew in Mary's
arms. Once you get stuck
in one—I mean labels
I won't kowtow to—
coming out is a difficult
affair. My preference
is for the edge, either
side of it will do! Our us.
It's fairly expected to see
what the results are. Who's
not gunning for those is
doomed to luff his sails,
and wherever I go, I bring
my own oars, on sea or on land.

# Susan Sontag

American author, cultural critic


i


And she dropped the ball of revolutionary change
when she had the greatest chance of effecting it,
when the Sixties came calling with its passionate
intensities and amoral propensities; to have gone
*there* would have required more than chasing out
the fixtures of the old hierarchies, it would have
entailed a self-transformation for the culture, for
the values of freedom and love she would later
abandon in favor of success and authority on the
national stage which she cultivated and relished.


ii


She wanted to bask in her
accomplishments as a public intellectual
and writer before dying.
Time finished her story too soon
but she parlayed her suffering into
troubles she could write about
without divulging their source—
isn't that the definition of writing,
to some extent: imposing distance
on an otherwise destabilizing
intimacy? Hers, nonetheless, fed
the pain she felt, and the pain she

inflicted, the confluence of which
spawned her writing as devotion
to truths she would interpret again
and again, that bodily falsified
itself without, at last, a body of work
to return to, to control, to create.

# Maggie Nelson

American writer

(her voice)   —after an interview 2017

Wholesale 'genius' I'm not, piecemeal maybe,
but it gets the job done, the term, used in
myriad contexts. I'll settle for the next big
thing, if the fates or the gods allow. I'm up
to my ears in thinking up new ways to slow
down, so I can get things done my way,
however it comes. I open the door to my
brain and out comes the little imp of an idea,
and I'm happy to follow him for a while. It's
a trail I like to get lost on, but not for too
long. I've got places to go, after all. And power
needed to get there won't stay forever. 'What's
up, doc?' is my favorite line, by the way, the rabbit
in me going for broke in every sentence I write.
Lovers inspire me, and I've had many. Marriage
being the routine I need to whip myself into shape,
I'm glad, and mad, about being a dad, mothering
my kids the way I want to. It's a story for the ages,
and I'll be the one to help tell it, too.
...Show's over, folks. It's been real.

# Cheryl Strayed

American writer

(her voice)   —after *Wild,* dir. Jean-Marc Vallee

None of the immigrants to this country, none,
came to these shores without a struggle.

Honestly, I was on the verge of starvation.
Roving off-road is what I came here to do.

Hunger had me at hello,
though I've died a thousand goodbyes.
Breath of a Martian travelled
a long distance to get here.

Time tames the wildness
out of us, but we endure
the same emptiness either way.

She loved me to my bones.
My mom built a castle of kindness
and everlasting devotion.
I'm walking to repay her
in some way, my way.
Vile storms I paid to get through.
Anger drove me to the
bottom of my life,
but at the pit of my stomach
I found a hunger to live.

She nailed existence in the deeps
with her love, and I wanted
to follow her there to know
what she felt, to feel what she knew.

Time cycles us out in due course.
But while we're on the move
we make time ours—to the beat
of two feet and a heart
pumping in a rhythm of
take & give, take & give.
My take on things, I must remind
you, takes a nothing I sense
is the source of my fear.
And power too.

You put down your Bowie knife
and who turns up commander-in-chief?
You can't risk it in this land.
We will supply the alternative
to spirits crushed to death out here.
Nature revives spirits here.

Her cancer led her to a place
where she knew she wouldn't live long.
The train tracks guide her journey
and she didn't want to get off.
Then she goes to town and forces
the doctors into making an admission
—you will soon die.

On the sex, baby, everybody can be tough.
Funny missing I'm here for.

# Patti Smith

American singer-songwriter

(her voice)

i       on playwright Sam Shepherd  i.m.


There is no blue deep enough
that does justice to the blueness
of his soul, let the crows peck
at the sky all they will, the crows
of the dead of night where he's gone.


ii      —after *Year of the Monkey*


The dream you want to have won't save
you from the waking reality you live,
but the sanguine acceptance of loss
has the picture in relative focus,
so you write from inside the heart
you call, not without misgivings, art.
Take away the solution and all you have
is the problem, holy now, and grave,
which the dream points to, a part
of the whole picture seen on the sly
before your friends and loved ones die.
Writing your way forward, you wave
to the future, knowing it, too, will lie.
Words, I swear, fall short as reply.

# Part Seven

*As with the stars,*
*you don't have to see*
*the scars, to know*
*that they're there.*

# Storyless

To be arriving perpetually at a place
that has no space, is no disgrace; to see
in your destination a destiny played out
in the sun-uplifted stars, is no fantasy
save one that has survived the drought;
to drink, then, at the fountain you behold
in a darkness deepening phase by phase
until at last the story gets told, is no mystery
wrapped in an enigma waiting to unfold.
To say of splendor that it has no home
is, by these lights, home enough if there be time.


To say what comes next is to undo
the said, soundly, which won't do
for said plot that we adhere to,
come what may. Ease up on the
plot restrictions, though, and the
whys and wherefores spill out
of their own accord, tangentially.
Still, it won't do to plot coordinates
all the way to the end, since every
word uttered, barring parallel
universes arising, makes its descent
of man the nominal story, once
for all, and not. The plot knows
where it wants to go, in other words,
even if we don't. Go figure.

Go deep enough, they say, and you'll find
the story that has meaning and resonance
beyond the ordinary lives we all lead. And
when you do, tell it slant, make it distant
from the emotions roiling about inside you.
Everyone has her or his story to tell, democracy's
truest form. But who will want to hear
yours depends on the third-person review
of events, not the first-person's, which holds
down the present but can't hold a candle
to the progress you, or your character self,
have otherwise made. No ordinary lives,
then, after all: but getting there is all.


A story always involves power. (But to be storyless
is to not be powerless.) Whatever happens next
is to be focused on and exploited. The arc
of narration is also the mark of predation.
Without a next to go to, anything goes.
Without a text to go to, nothing stays.
Hence History's linear motion conquers
the Soul's descent. What if, however,
the Self is by nature dialogic, the Double
seeking give and take rather than denouement.
The very word 'climax' reveals the sexual
act as intrinsic to the power of the story.
No climax, no story. No story, no power.
Story is sexy because it has places to go.
Storyless endures by oscillation, no direction home
except through separation, transition, and reintegration.

Who will be there to record
the passing of events, the world
receding into dim recollection,
the mind's predilection
to match nature an untold
story seeking resolution,
sources hidden in plain sight
give or take the bottomless night.


No interaction of consequence is played
without rules of the game. Had I stayed,
I would have learned them, the rules,
for you who can see how it fools
he who thinks the day is won, but fades
to where there's nothing but ghouls
that haunt, as night vanishes into shade…

# Keith Botsford

—American/European writer   i.m.

i (his voice) —after a YouTube interview, 2013

The luck of the Botsfords having run out,
I sit at my desk smoking Galoises, greasing
the wheels of the ego I'm spinning out
of words in French, comporting myself
as the doyen I always wanted to be.

ii  (his voice) —after *Fragments II*

My life had to be written down, being
a good journo myself. The rich have their
mouths perennially open—to what exactly?
Hunger of a sort that can never be assuaged,
which drew me in like a spider its prey. My
mother sat square in the center of that web,
forever ensnared by it, and I've been trying
all my life with words to un-ensnare her, and
myself, from that giant web of deception.
My brother had an ease and charm that made
the web alluring. As for me, I wanted in
and out both at the same time, happy from
the outside to write as if an insider. Where
I belonged, to this day I don't know. She,
my mother, kept the ruse up all her life, that
her place in the web was pre-ordained, even
if at her expense. My father, meanwhile,

drifted in and out before finally leaving her
for good, sparing none of us the shock of
his infidelity. But three marriages later
I see all this and write it down, imagining
details that I can't remember, savoring
the memories of a time long since past
that I'd bring back to life one scene at a time,
a Hollywood film by any other name, edited
and reworked not necessarily for the
record but for Babylon, for fame.

iii


…Yes, the history I have has me in its hands,
if not by the throat, and I, gasping for air,
note the ground beneath me falling away
until now I'm sailing on a boat on a sea
where the waves, now becalmed, now choppy,
now cresting, sweep me toward newer shores.

# History X

Environment and experience, no matter
how uneventful or unimportant they may
seem at the time, are all one really has by
which to define oneself, by which has been
constructed historical man. But what of
factors unseen, behind appearances?
What of, as it were, *cosmic man*?

...On that day
the spirit world
descended and made
itself known to him...

to find a way to write the autobiographical
by constructing desire, instead of a gestalt self,
a matrix of interconnected relationships
and interactions with multiple selves—
a cognitive shift, as citizen of the noosphere—
the mirroring the constellation does wordlessly,
can be seen in the depths...

The thought on the furthest
node of your brain still resonates
inside, where you hear
a voice—whose?—in sharp
utterance amid the static of
incoming waves.

The power dynamics are fluid
and, in some cases, unpredictable.
Insistence on authority alternates
with a willingness to cooperate
with the reader in the poem's
creation of meaning. Power cannot
last long in a vacuum, however.

To be a channel is to be assimilated
into territory that, once written, is already lost.

But soulful artists touching the underground
world, is the issue. It doesn't matter when, not if,
the lords of the above take over the territory.

These are tiniest instances,
pieces of moments.

What did you think I wanted?

The Japanese house,
you can't live in them.
Just as the world has no
concern with Asian politesse
or forms of social interaction
viewed as quaint or exotic.

The drumroll of quick magic.

The bark is worse than
the bite! Come on then!
Live a little! Realize your dreams.

Transcendental is on the rise.
It's how to make it with

these bodies—girls and boys.

Never tells you what to say
Never tells you what to do

When the sound of
your inner bones are
cracking in your ears.

Counterlife resonated.

The man has addled on his brain.

The flake wrote a fluke
of a book and took
flak for it.

Accessed simplicity
for harrowing complexity.

High and low
his flow took him.

Took a hit
as a poet.
Would mate
with his muse,
whatever the
going rate.
Called it fate.

Here... as... history...
of... bloody... Babylon...

# Christopher Plummer

—after *Remember*, dir. Atom Egoyan

(his voice)

The way you looked at me
kind of said, Look down.
Down. Look down.

The logjam of feelings
is released.
We store them up
over a lifetime.

Daring is needed
to do the deed.
Punishment and revenge
for the misdeeds of
the past, unremembered,
of which I'm here to remind you.

Honor among thieves, you say?
I'm no thief, I'm your
conscience come for judgment day.

We blame the tears, fears & years
that have held us back
from remembering who
we really are—the name
you once had, the self you hid away.

The Nazi boot sole on
the Jewish backside
was more or less permanent
after Kristallnacht. Out
of it came a plan for
the Jews to lose their culture,
their wealth & property, and
finally, their lives.
You become as valued as disease.

…When we moved to Scotland
I did not want the winter to be
long, a room with a view,
angels of snow rustling up as snow.

# Arab Spring

(early 2010s)   (their voices)

Tanks roll down
boulevards of freedom;
we won't play dumb.
We won't let
the atmosphere of fear
trample on our rights.

Ample revolutionary implosions
to be found in history,
but we won't budge
from our place in it.

The Egyptian VP looks out only for himself,
carefully laying the groundwork to snuff out
the movement of revolutionary upheaval.
Renewal is the force he is threatened by,
and trying to thwart. Guard your tactic
of non-violence, for your survival depends on it.

Anguish will come, you must be brave
in the face of cruelty. In this is your defense
against overwhelming odds. The forces
arraying against you behind the scenes
will soon be unleashed. God protect you.

Will America have the blood of young martyrs
on its hands, for all of time?

The world is watching and waiting.

Alleviate suffering is the first tenet of brotherhood.

Come to the aid of the future, or it will die, and you with it.

The revolutionary movement is arrayed
like a David against the Goliath of the state.
The stand it makes in Liberation Square
for all to see, echoes that of the Spartans
against the Persian army juggernaut.
Do they stand a chance?

Remember your ties. You are satellites
of the sun of hope of justice. Let your call
be heard and infamy come
to those who would silence it.

Tears to come, may you sow the ground
of the next generation. May you stand
tall though you may fall. Yours
is the voice of all who have come
through hell to tell of hope and freedom.

Don't think you will not please.

Mubarak and his henchmen have put in place
forces around the country. They will attack,
and families of demonstrators will also be targeted.

*

Heinous crimes about to be committed

against the Egyptian protesters.
Edelweiss my ass! Cows being led
to the slaughter. Beware.

Step into the fray?
'Make my day' is
what the cops all say.

Taking the swells
of history is what they
will end up doing.

Let them be,
they'll turn into
a curiosity, they said.
Now look at the tiger
that's been unleashed.

Behind the scenes
Hell awaits you.

America fights for
her interests.
Egypt fights for
her dignity.

The voice, it says—
No, I'm not going to change,
unless the world in me changes.

Egypt. It was about calling
the powerful to account.

Rebirth is what
the long struggle
is about—your own.

Civil unrest is no lame gesture
to the politics of namelessness.
What wants saying gets said
by the bodies of the dead
or those willing to die.
There is no greater cry
from either heart or spleen.
The action a people's pain takes
insists on reaction from
the deaf state of affairs.

(Libya)
Destruction of bodies—removing
the dead & hiding the evidence:
Now the dead are not worth
the time of day.

*

Egypt and Syria and Arab Spring are
expressions of revolutionary movements
that don't die out—they reappear
in different form and different time elsewhere.

# Paris Terror

—aftermath of Paris terrorist attacks, November, 2015

(their voices)

We have prepared the day
with the night's abyss peered
into. What have we seen of it
to teach us the next steps, we
wonder. Where will these next
steps lead? We abjure the fear
that would reverse our course.
We defy those who, with abominable
tactics, would darken our lives
with terror. Undone by death are
the many we now mourn. Lady
Liberty, blindfolded no more, turns
now to face the war waged against
us, the one sown over the last
thousand years… Perilous are the
times ahead. God for whom we
fight, and country, will unite.
Through the cracks of the crumbling
edifice of the West will come its
destroyers. Forewarned is forearmed
is the swath now being cut across
history to upend the direction it's
been taken. No future is secure.
Shibboleths to be brought down
are ones that say the West is

invincible, that it represents the best
of humanity, and that it offers
the only viable path forward.
Feel the ground of that narrative
shift beneath your feet as radical
Islam tries to seize control of events
to alter the story you tell yourselves.
Ours is the story of the ages: that
there is no God but Allah, and
The West will shudder in our
shadow before long. The 'better
day' is ours, meanwhile, to claim.

*


Armed to fight to the end,
they showed no mercy in
bringing the battle to them.

Anger boils over in capitals of
the western world, with nobody
coming right out and saying so.

Tomorrow brings with it
the price of today. What's clear
is there's no way clear of
the mess we've made. We—
the West—will be learning
this lesson for centuries to come.

Challenge of our age is to
be able to contain the changes.

We haven't the stomach for the fight
being taken to us, is the fear.

Atlas needed for the new world must
include the mouse the cat dragged in
who sniffs his way out of his bind
to say, 'Cheese.'

Nobody can say what will come next,
all bets are off the table.

Problems? The place will be
crawling with them now.
Years in the waiting, the wait's no more.

Some of you said the stomach is ill-fitted
for the fight ahead—this all has to be
digested from now, on a moment's notice.
The balance of power shifts for more war,
and a terrible one it will be.

The weapons tree will grow huge.

Step forward into the morass we'll
all be in the middle of, before long.

We got shot in the neighborhoods—please
close the panorama while we heal.

Someone had to give, and we did.
From the gift that keeps killing.

How to prepare the world for
the blindness that no one wants to see?

Inshallah, wages war on the peace
that never was.

*

We fan out in all directions into the breach
of terror and violence, only to find witnesses
to the event on the streets of the city
stepping forward in defiance. We see in their eyes
the smoldering look of having survived,
and the courage to continue at all odds.
The city is under siege but normal, too,
to a certain extent which it will never
truly be again normal. But teeth are
gritted and people go forward as if
it will be just another day.

# Noam Chomsky

American linguist, critic

(his voice)

What the U.S. holds is not just power
vis-a-vis its material wealth, it holds
capital—social, intellectual, artistic—
in hock to corporations that run the nation,
a new kind of governance, one to which
we are all beholden, like it or not.
The U.S. President executes people
abroad in illegal drone warfare that
has no precedent, nor, for that matter,
moral backbone. It's disingenuous to say
America stands by its democratic ideals
when corporate interests come
first before the people's. We are also
running out of time in our age of
declining empire—though perhaps old age
makes kicking oneself in the butt into
a worldview. Nonetheless we cannot
procrastinate with regards the perilous threats
we face—nuclear war and environmental
disaster. The future has never been under
such threat as now, and we must do
something about it before it's too late.

# Howard Zinn

American historian

(his voice)

Stripped of our moral certainties of America's
exceptionalism, we're left with the city on the hill
that can no longer serve as a model for others.
That city exists to hold up a superiority
we can no longer claim, if we ever could.
Our idea of American exceptionalism sold us
a bill of goods no right-minded person should trust.

*

Back door politics opened a trapdoor
into the underside of what America thought
itself to be, and there was no going back,
threatening to swallow America's
exceptionalism in the bargain.

# Julian Assange

Australian editor, whistleblower

Assange dares do the dirty work
despite risking thought of as a dickhead.
Being misunderstood is part of the trouble
he's brought upon himself,
but he doesn't shy from a fight.
He embraces it, rather, to a fault.
And therein lies his flaw,
tragic by his lights, but one
that gives him, he believes, gravitas,
a persona for the ages.
Not a wannabe actor but a player
in the field of change, at least
as he sees himself. And the world
opinion he courts is partly to blame.
Silence is golden in heaven,
but not here on earth.
The un-sainted precincts of politics
requires a bullhorn to be effective.
That's where Wikileaks comes into play.
Is it to make his name, or
to save the lives of countless others—
you be the judge. The jury is still out.
He rocks and rolls to the tune
of death metal and the blues,
jazzing up the proceedings with
a rough-hewn charisma and
a full-blown ego fit for the stars.

Take away that ego and what have you
got left—a whistleblower's dream
in a nightmare world.

# Derrick Jensen

American environmentalist

i

The writings of the writer who
denounces violence are rife with violence
(go figure). Close your eyes and see
massacre after massacre that inform his (our)
own wounded imagination and seeds
perhaps more violence down the line.
Beware, his work indirectly declares,
the moral high ground. For it won't
protect you from violence itself. He
announces our shadow and how it
moves across the dying earth.

ii  American landscape (post-Parkland)

The gun-toters have left us in tatters.
We ache with that heartbreak
at the edge of reason, waiting
to be acquitted of treason,
(the right to arm may as well be
the right to harm), while healing
leaves us wheeling in a circle round.
A moving target we'll be caught up to
one day, the trigger pulled far
out of sight of our exit wound.

# Edward Snowden

American author, whistleblower

The man who left behind his 'free country'
wondering how the moral compass of
so many around him had failed; the man
who, by his account, entered the labyrinth
of identity only to discover multiple selves
adding up to, in another's words, a gentle
cipher uninterested in convincing you of his
uniqueness; the man expatriated to Russian soil
for perhaps the remainder of his days, fated
to live as a foreigner, a stranger, an outlaw;
the man who remade himself in the image
of a whistleblower following his conscience
and the revered Constitution—is a man,
his *Permanent Record* notwithstanding,
who as fugitive may end up being forgotten.

# Barack Obama

44th American president


(his voice) —after a conversation w/ Marilynne Robinson
2015


Here I am, the President of the United States,
speaking with a novelist, one I deeply respect,
a novelist of ideas as well as of characters, and
I'm wondering how I can raise the level of discourse
for whoever may read this conversation, to lift it up
a bit, so democracy can be showcased in a better light,
a light that personifies our differences without belittling
the otherness that is the fabric of our existence,
that we wear as history, as philosophy, as law, as
economics, as politics. So this conversation can steer us
over dangerous landscapes as well, with what it means
to be American in a time of backlash and pushback
against those liberal values we hold dear, ones which
have served us well in my term in office and that have
helped shape the national agenda in spite of what can be
construed as conspiracy to derail those values. It's what
we've talked about before this meeting, but do the American
people know, I wonder, and would it fly in the face of norms
we live by to harbor ill-will against those people, and you know
who I'm talking about. Or would it be better if we just move on
and stay optimistic, since I feel that's what will get us to
the next summit, the next proper alignment of spiritual and
political values that my daughters and your sons may depend on,
that's how I see the trials of my two terms and what they've

taught me. I don't want to let the American people down,
I don't want to let my family down, and here we are talking
about the future as we see it not from some ivory tower but
from the cornfields and small towns of the Midwest where
who we are as a nation has been nourished. It's food for
moral clarity that I can't get enough of, for which I am grateful.
It's an elevated place I aspire to, and we can take many others
along for the ride and hopefully will be better for it.
So thank you for going along with me.

# Marilynne Robinson

American novelist

(her voice)

It won't last, the furor we face
over what's given to us by grace,
and whether it's deserved or not;
still, we have no choice but to fight
our way through the uncertainties
that in life are inevitable, as our lot,
and woe betide us for shirking mysteries
called time and space, history's
plot by any other name, the pair lined up
in circular fashion with what opens us up,
heart-wise, to the wonders of the pale blue dot
we live and die on, as I see it.

# Journo-Interviewer

(her voice)  2016

This guy's rich in fun, as well
as in billions of dollars, and
what that brings to the table
no one is yet sure of, but love
women he does, scarily even,
if a former beauty pageant owner
tells us anything. I've won
my right to report the news
without being subject to come-
ons from presidential hopefuls
who, if truth be told, puts fun
on equal footing in the conversation.
It's new terrain we're walking on,
we female reporters. He may be done.
He may not. The run he makes
on power, though, old as he is,
is going to be loads of fun!...

# Political Journo

— post-election day America, 2016

(his voice)

The possible has never seemed more threatening,
now that Trump's in the driver's seat. His world
will crash before long, and ours with it, so we
brace ourselves. Some of us will fight to steer
us away from the catastrophe that others see
is sure to come. We have our ideals to think of,
here in the USA, but they are rapidly going down
the drain of vituperation, vindictiveness, and
vicious bigotries. Woe betide us to ignore the
signs, and they are legion, as are the voters who
put him in charge. The TV personality as president
coming next. Stay tuned.

# **Political Commentaries**

— circa 2016

Shoehorn politics into
mainstream agendas,
The Donald wins
coming or going.
The People—that's
another matter entirely.

The shoals watch out for.
We don't want
The Ship of State floundering, but
neither can we expect
smooth sailing. It's all
hands on deck, and full steam ahead!

A knife fight—
Which one is yours,
which one is mine.

I cut off my body
to save my head.

You mean the United States
is ready to shard its most
cherished rights?

*

What issue made Trump
into such a crappy politician?

A lot of bad news.

He thinks the media
will bend to his will.

He's no ordinary politician.
He rolls from the gut.

We're humans. That means
we'll fight the Trump and
Hillary in us no matter who
we are. Even if we're Hillary
and Trump themselves.

*

Associative thought trumps logical
thought in the political arena, as in
mostly elsewhere, but it also courts
disaster in its unpredictability and invites
demagoguery in its pandering to fear
and prejudice. Intuition plays on
improvisatory tactics in the constantly
moving stream of events real-time,
whereas Logic builds an armor of
thought and an edifice of organization.
Trump, it turned out, has a genius
for the former, and with those instincts
on full throttle, blew out of the water the latter.

The tide of human events
swept a monster into power.
God help America, god help
the world.

We not only got crazy,
we got sublime.
Trump's America.

# Political Journo

(his voice)  —after *The New York Times,* 2017

The signs point to a debacle
of the century. Yet how can
we live without hope? Trump
won't trump hope if the people
have any say. And we do! Get
out there and make your voices
heard, is the only way forward
now. The rest is off the table
that nobody's sitting around
anymore, but are instead fixated
on their smartphone screens
texting one another ad nauseum.
Not even Facebook counts for
much anymore. The rules are
being re-written as we speak,
and it's not going to be pretty.
Collateral damage already in—
immigrants who want in are
on their way out, the judge's
staying order notwithstanding.
We're seeing a naked disregard
of the norms of governance for
maximum effect—play to the
political base and keep a straight
face, an agenda bent on undoing
constitutionally protected rights
and installing stooges and puppets

to run the show. No one's exempt
from the cynicism and contempt
coming down the pike for real
the next four years.

# Ron Rosenbaum

*The Los Angeles Times* writer

(his voice) 2017

The done deal Trump wants us to accept
is far from done. The bald lie that Trump
wants us to believe is far from bald. We crave
our spot in the sun, and he'll be the one
to give it to us, he claims. We, the nameless
hordes, the pot of gold of the demagogue,
rush in where angels fear to tread, but
are dead to the machinations used to get
us to trot to his tune, the music of fear.
We must not be cowed, not now, not ever,
by the abuse of not just the Constitution
but of basic human decency that will
stain this period of American history
like no other. Mark my words—unless
we mark the words of truth-tellers in
the press, we'll have no democracy to
speak of, cowed into silence we'll be.
The roar of the people, however, must be
heard. The mouse of the people devoured
otherwise.

# Adam Gopnik

*The New Yorker* staff writer

i   (his voice) 2017


It won't be for lack of truth-telling
that we fall into the flytrap of lies
our president has set for the country.
The buck stops here, with each of us
proof positive that a sane world exists
despite evidence to the contrary.
Make no mistake, we face a perversion
of not just democratic norms but of
the bedrock values that we hold dear.
Were we to give an inch Trump not
only will take a mile, he'll take the
shirts off our backs with a smile.
This con will go down in history
as contempt for democracy's We:
His is constant upkeep of a royal I
that, if left uncriticized, will erode
the foundations on which we stand.
What passes for truth is no passing lie
but reality's bulwark dangerously unmanned.
It's up to us to defend it unequivocally.


ii   (his voice) 2017


He shreves the remnants of democratic
parlance with not just lies but obfuscation

that informs every utterance, until Trump
and his coterie stand for self-enrichment
in the face of continuing but ineffective
scrutiny, since what he does and is are
of a pair: twisted lie and befouled cry
of rulers who would render the rule of law
moot. We press the mute button on the show
at our own peril. Watch we must, if only
to feel the sting of corruption in our depths,
and maybe to take up arms against it,
which is what it may come to, alas.


*


Trump reveals himself to be a wimp
with a wagging finger that, when
offended, can push the button to launch
missiles and kill countless others in distant
lands, and woe betide us to believe otherwise.
For this is a president of truly random evil.


iii    (his voice) 2020


Times take our crisis seriously—
called 'whither democracy?'—
in a continual loop, a republic
threatened by the rot from within
and the autocratic tendencies
humans in every era give in to.
So defend her we must, by small,
boring measures on behalf of institutions
that keep her afloat, without which
she would sink. And we with her.

# Political Journo

(his voice)

I don't see how the White House
is anything but stress, ego-driven stress.
What will get us out of this mess
won't reveal itself anytime soon,
I'm afraid. We're in it for the long
haul of epic proportions, a Capt. Ahab-like,
manically driven commander-in-chief
who's on course to bring the whole
Ship of State down with him. Only
the thick-skinned among us stand
a chance of surviving this, and even
then there are no guarantees. Lord
have mercy on our souls, if
we had them, that is.

But why should we give it to the country,
our allegiance?

Because, as its citizens we owe it.

*

Trump still play acts,
play acts, play acts.
The world will remember
him as a clown.

*

One human, one world.

Guarding it like
a fox, his seized power.

Now in America
all bets are off.

Sycophants and yes-men
surround the president.

Shell—
I am hardened by the sea,
smoothed by the sand,
and hollowed out
by time.

The death of profit
and incentive.

Numbers crunching time.

The ring finger
gives way to
the middle finger,
and Americans vote
thumbs up, or down.

*

Why would I do something
courageous like that?

Mozart—
the intricacy of his music
takes you to the stars.

The times not only are dark,
they are grotesque.

What a martini
should taste like!

Mechanism in place
intended to kick in
during a crisis,
utterly failed.

# Barton Gellman

*The Atlantic* writer,  Dec. 2021

(his voice)

Climb the ramparts and what do we see?
A democracy fading into the night, closely
followed by the flag our fathers fought for,
an America taken down by an angry mob
fueled by voter suppression and gerry-
mandering that will stack the odds in their
favor the next time around, an election
stolen right out from under us, being planned
as we speak, while the country looks on
in disbelief, and the president flinches
in the face of the dire threat posed by
his enemies, a threat they'll make good on
to usher in the Trump Era Redux, you'll see.

# George Packer

*The Atlantic* writer, Dec. 2021

(his voice)

Times they are a-changing, and for the worse,
if truth be known, were anybody listening. We
cannot afford to rest but must fight as only
the left in alliance with the center-right can—
with a vision of moderation and a foundation
of can-do spirit on behalf of our democracy
precious for being two hundred fifty years old
and counting, if we don't lose it in the next
election heading our way, one without fail-
safes in place to protect the will of the people.
The imagination needed for this battle
will test our endurance to the limit, but
there is no other choice, else we face
democracy's, and America's, demise.

# Morgan Gibson

American expatriate poet, critic   i.m. 2017

i   (his voice)

Alan, the high tide of filth that Trump
floats in on will, in the proper order
of things, be replaced by the low tide
of true solidarity, the so-called gathering
of the tribes I have in mind to launch myself
upon in my old age. Doddering I'm not yet,
keen I still am to report what I find.
It's of a kind you're bent on, too, I sense.
So let us break bread together and make
headway against life's incoming storms.
We shall make of our time what we will:
The proper ordering of mind and body
being the soul's proper task, if you ask me.
Such, alas, is the task I set for myself as
I negotiate the end, or is it the beginning
as Walt would say—that great-souled one
you rode piggy-back on, and right you did
by him, too, never mind the nay-sayers.
The Yes grows by leaps and bounds by virtue
of Walt-like generosities I can't afford
not to make room for anymore. Poetry
limited, can only take one so far. Raise
the bar your book has done, challenging
anyone to take it to heart, a dare I accept
full-heartedly. Caring for others is the first

order of business, mind you. Then
we shall see what we shall see…
If the purpose of life is to light the lampwick
for others to see by, I'm all in.


ii  (his voice)


Alan-san has hands down cornered
the market on waging battles unseen
that fallow fields are sown by, the dead
having ceded no territory other than
wisdom earned the hard way, to be
harvested in dreams the future brings.
Love he sings in spades, not separate
from the soil he roots in, to blossom
anywhere at any time, past one's prime
if necessary, that old age looks back on
fondly and recalls, a world at a rhyme.
We correspond, he and I, as twins do—
arm in arm, hand in hand, eye to eye—
a history-making plot I've lain in
and stood up for, that here and there,
above and below, the twain do meet
in sound sense construed in innocence,
he branching upward to the light, and
I spreading rootward into night.
What I see and what he sees converge
in energies of the processional, but diverge
in energies of the confessional. As is, words
bodily heard, though eerie impediments
be admitted, true minds encompass:
the inner accountant tallies, the inner
lawyer litigates, and the inner critic

judges. Still, no closer are we to the truth
as we see it, but that it sees us, a matter
of imagination's viewing heaven on earth.


iii  (his voice)


The future beckons, and where I'll
be I can't say. That'll be the day,
however, when I go back
to the U.S. of A. It ain't what
it used to be, and I'm not exaggerating
when I say it's Redneck City across
the country, now that Trump's in
the driver's seat. And it'll never
be the same again. What's in a name,
indeed, but the country's been trumped,
or at least the one I knew. Don't be
a stranger. We're neighbors now.
The hayseeds of the land have spread,
taken to fertile soil, though the
proverbial needle in a haystack that
a poem has become, for me, I won't
go searching for. My days of poetry
writing are done. Now it's how
the East has won, my loyalties if
not my affection. Little else to do
but watch the shambles going on
across the pond. The wound of
the world, Alan, widens with age.


*

Loss you've made a game of,
or appear to have.

Loss is the boss of us all,
gloss it all we will.
Gold-diggers, too, who corner
the market on dross,
as we both know,
anamolies notwithstanding.

Here's the ugly side of loss—
it never comes back, or not
as you'd expect it. The boss
of loss, then, is art,
art that converts loss
either to gold or to dross.

iv

The dire exigencies of old age
come upon those of us known
or unknown, and how we cope
with them takes the measure
of a person, for the arrow of time
targets us all.

# The Day George H. W. Bush Died

I dreamed I was in the hallway
of an apartment building when
a tall, thin middle-aged white man
appeared with his friendly dog,
which I petted, before he opened
the door to his apartment and
invited me in. We walked past
cluttered rooms until we reached
a place in the back. Wait till you
see this, he said. The room lay
spread before me, covered with
buildings from one end to the other,
a model city teaming with possibilities
I had never considered, unhaunted
by the fallen, clear as the sky
I could not see. He stood proudly
above it all, and with a sweep
of his hand, I woke up.

*


He looks at it
in a very important way.

Creative in a way
the waking mind can
never be.

Life can change on a dime,
or by pennies from heaven.

The U.S. is not in a position
to offer moral lessons to anyone.

If every word we muttered
mattered, imagine how
we'd live our lives.

See that rose over there?
Embrace the rose.

He went south
with his mouth
He went forth
to the north
for the yeast
of the east.
The rest is
the west.

What kind of world do I live in?
Nobody lives in it but me.

Every act
gets written
down in history
as you're living it.

The question is,
who will read it?

What you see
is a mystery
that you can't see
in history.

The rain, the wind, the bird.

# Another Country

In my dream this morning
(whose dream is it, anyway?)
it seemed I was trying to find my way
back (it often happens, my getting lost)
to where I started from, but I lack
the wherewithal until something
turns up, and I'm on my way
(it could be a horse, or a truck, or a plane)
but before I reach the place
I'm headed for with all my effort
I wake up, you could say to the reality
of my life, finding myself in real time wondering
why the dream felt so true, so real
that I believed it heart and soul,
until I realize that home
is always what I'm one dream
away from, and I'm
always, wherever I am, on my way,
like when I see the foreigner pray
at the shrine, bowing his head
and clapping his hands, I know
the strangeness will last,
but the unbelonging I feel won't.
For it's earth where I spend
my days with you that's
the truth, that's
the dream.

# Part Eight

*The stones are much harder*
*the stars are much brighter*
*when a person feels free*

# Brenda Goodman

i  American painter   (her voice)

Nine times out of ten my paintings
begin at surrendering my will to
my unconscious. There it begins
to take on a life of its own, growing
on its own terms, becoming what I
can't recognize as my own, but I
follow it anyway to see where it
takes me, so the journey is one of
discovery, if I'm lucky.


ii  John Yau, American critic  (his voice)

She's taken the vows of painting
and for 50 years she prays in color
and line and shapes. I admire her
strangeness and fearlessness in
the face of it, that others would
turn away from but she embraces
fully. I can't read her paintings as
a fixed destination at all. She invites
irregular pathways and disturbing
itineraries to arrive at a certain
power of her life's inner meaning.
She won't box it out but lets it
emerge…

iii   —after nude 'Self-portrait'   (her voice)


Most people are free
to make freedom fail.
It's a wish that accomplishes
a place you can trust, an accident
is the start and I see how you
answer the nude book,
the nude women brainstorming
leading the way.

# Camille Paglia

American cultural critic

i        (her voice)  —after *Provocations*

I dialed up controversy and doubled down
on contrariness to feed my appetite for battle.
Make no mistake, a woman needs weapons, not
slogans, to get her where she wants to go. Hail
Mary my soul to keep will get you only so far.
The umbrage taken by so-called feminists
rings hollow to my ears, and always has. Fuel
for future skirmishes soon to come my way
can be found in my latest book, a sexual
politics tome spanning my career. Dear
readers, hail the fire and brimstone it contains
and you'll see all hell breaking loose. Recluse
I'm not, just an excuse to dabble in my passion
of late, Indian arrowhead digging and the like.
Woeful the barometric readings are of the nation
I love. If the shit-storms coming our way are
Trump's fault, I'll eat my hat! They've been
a long time brewing, if you must know, and
I don't see storm shelters worth fleeing to.
Au contraire, best to steer straight into the
winds, ill or not, and that includes the slings
and arrows of misfortune, which are sure
to arrive, as Mary is my witness. Balance
in the face of them, and counter-attack are
my preferred tactics. Anything less is career
suicide. We women making common cause

to stick it to the Man, is not a fight I want
to join. Patriarchy patronizes, it's true, but
matriarchy infuses the culture with over-wrought
wiles where outright confrontation is called for.
At least in my book. Coming soon to a store near you!

ii  (her voice)

The accolades I got I deserved, punching
my way as I did into the cultural maelstrom.
We—and I mean proto-feminists, whether
first or second wave—still have everything
to prove, in opposition to the campus police
state undoing the free speech we fought
valiantly for. Wherefore art thou, Romeo?
The Juliets of our time are bent on maligning
and marginalizing the male gender, they to
whom we owe for the construction of modern
civilization. I offer dissent from the mainstream
culture coddling students on campus. Women's
power must be reclaimed at every turn, not
allowed to be relinquished to thought police
and their usurping post-structuralist laws.

iii  (her voice)

Cantankerous I must be to battle
the cant I see and hear around me
in so-called cultural discourse. I can't
ignore it. Bring it on, I say, and I'll
have my say heard, come what may!
The Dolly Partons of the world won't
hold sway in the world I live and breathe

in, the one I'd help create and refine,
since that's what I trained myself for—
to get into the front lines and mix it up
and do battle over ideas, for the right
to express myself and to be heard over
the culture's noise—and it's loud, believe
me! One has got to shout to get heard,
unfortunately, since that's where we are
in America, the louder you shout, the
higher your ratings. But I want to be heard
on the merits of my thinking, my ideas
leading the way, syncretic thought,
to be sure, yet anything but uptight!
I'm for the mind's liberation, the sooner
the better, the more the merrier! Without
liberatory prospects, the mind gets impaled
on dogma and ideology, when what it needs
most is liberation and expansion, and the
wherewithal to live those terms, not be
cowed by the difficult truths they reveal.
This is what I'm after, and nothing culturally
can be accomplished before as many minds
as possible are liberated and empowered
through rigorous if evanescent clamor
that is the mind's—the generous mind's—
signature, its natural bailiwick that all
great thinkers give wide berth to. Am I
one of them? I'll let you decide!


iv  artist exemplar  (her voice)


To let loose in the modern era is the aim
of the filmmaker, who has at his disposal

marvels of technological invention hitherto
unknown to artists. George Lucas is the
artist par exemple, who defines the meaning
of true innovator with stunning visualizations
of battle and human emotion projected on
the silver screen. His dance-like choreography
of men and machines renders the screen into a
palpitating, constantly metamorphizing stage
visualized in three dimensions. No one who
has ever seen the *Star Wars* series can ever
view movies the same way again, in terms
of imaginative breadth and technological
inventiveness in the service of a story-myth.


v  a theory of beauty  (her voice)


I to I is the mission of man,
while woman shadows the truth
it beholds. We yearn to connect
by projection as male dominance
female acceptance misses by a
mile and then some. We shy
from our truths, then, in order
to not be swallowed by them.
Staged, thus, is the battle of
the sexes—fornication the
drama behind closed doors we
let our imaginations loose by.
Harrowing the dilemma sex
foists upon us, but we parlay
its terrors into manageable fantasies
that allow us to acclimatize to
the mysteries themselves without

ever solving them. The mysteries
of sex as power and vice versa.
Love we need, however, for the
construction of the drama that
keeps us coming back, a return
to our senses once we take leave
of our minds. The chthonian
frenzy we fear as devouring, acts
as a force on the back of which
we ride hellbent to otherness,
to be consummated sexually as
Providence. Hell is no place we
see, and every place we go, by
the mother tongue which our
heavenly father vouchsafes us,
redeemable by neither love nor art
but as history's dream all the same.

vi  (her voice)

The girdle my mother wore
the girls of my generation swore
off with a vengeance, and now
we pole dance front and center
stage for all to see and admire.
It's what I call intellectual porn,
where stirring desire is fantasy-
fueled power of female sexuality
about which we've torn off shackles
and released—hormones et al—
into the mainstream with a ferocity
unlike anything the culture has ever
seen before. Where this power will

take women, depends upon factors
still coming into play. Ideas for
the new millennium I have on offer
will help rev things up, to be sure,
but the surge that must follow it
I aim to bring about. What
I'm fighting for is nothing less.
Let the world be warned—women's
power is here to stay, will not be
stripped away, will in due course
seize the day, and my say in getting
us there, to the fray I do thee wed,
is a marriage made in hell, Eros
by any other name, heaven be damned!


vii  (her voice)


The world is burning beyond my control
but as I see things, I still have a role
to play, so I speak out for the civilization
threatened on all sides—the one men built
as extensions of their pride and bliss.
Is this not what gets their creative juices
flowing, driven to invent a better way, contra
Mother Nature and her imperious suspense
of the rational? Gender wars, too, have
led us into infernal territory, but the gay
swerve from nature is evidence of adaptation
that supplants, as it were, natural selection.
Islam I've mostly shied from, due to perilous
notions in the West of cultural superiority.
Those waters I refuse to wade far in, for fear
of drowning in a clash of civilizations I, for one,

remain ill at ease with. Besides, how the West was won
is the operative phrase here, which I'll do my part
to defend in my writings on culture and art.
Seers, meanwhile, at the edges of society grant us
visions we'd do well to explore, is my take—
everything else is mostly fake.


*


…The weaker side of me
thought things could
change quickly.

# Laura Kipnis

American cultural critic


(her voice)      —after *Unwanted Advances*


What women have gained they've lost again
in the crosswinds to getting to where they'd been
twenty years earlier, or so we'd believed.
Now the onus is on us to begin redefining
the boundaries that need protecting, guarding
against the very real threats, and those perceived
threats, that are eating up our freeedoms. We
cannot go back again yet must close the gap
between us and them, yes and no, until
agency is upheld, protocols understood,
and everyone can just get along. Not.
Still, the advances made cannot be unmade
without our giving them away, so it's
incumbent upon us women to claim our rights
and cede no more ground unnecessarily.
Ours, then, will be the hat-trick of the age—
to respect women, to honor difference,
and to shine our light in the darkness.

# Laura Poitras

American film director

(her voice)    —after *Risk*

In time, the doers best the talkers.
So in the end, what can we produce?
What is the bottom line
of our ideas and values?
Faith-based corporate takeover
of the mass media bodes ill
for our democracy.

Can you give us the reason why
you trusted Assange?

Like I said, he's a doer
not a talker, and he holds
power in the realm of action.
I found that his actions—
the far-reaching effects of his actions—
speak for themselves.
They don't oversell the goods.
The deeds can speak volumes.
We're living under the shroud
of the surveillance state, which
is taking down the pillars of our
democracy—free speech and the
first amendment right to it. No one
wants to risk blowing the whistle

anymore because they know
the price paid is too high. We've
lost the foundations of our freedom.
Crammed like a kernel bent in a corner
without sunlight or water, the growth
of our democracy will be stunted
for years to come. Tie all our words
into a bundle and still all you've got
is a sack of words. Action, though,
is sexier, bolder—it gets things moving,
at times risking all.

# Oprah Winfrey

American media owner, television host

(her voice) —after Golden Globes speech 2018

Go tell it on the mountain speech
should knock them dead.
I've beat the odds to get here
and will prove my mettle still to come.
It's a winner I aim to show them,
come from the losing side of the tracks.
I've nothing to hide. We Americans
are greatness-obsessed, but I don't
want to make it great again, I just
want great to be the operative word
for who we are, as a people, for all,
white folk and black folk alike. Then
the system we challenge won't fear
us, but will hear us. The front parlor
will do nicely, chairs for everyone.
…Now you listen to me. I practically
invented 'compassion'. And I own
'empathy'. They're part of my brand.
Empowering others I do blindfolded,
don't anybody tell me about empowering.

# Lady Gaga

American singer, actress

(her voice)   —after *A Star is Born*, dir. Bradley Cooper

Make a girl happy,
tag with me.
Your part to play finds
me as a future star.
All the signs add up to it
and the crazy part is
we don't have friends.
We don't be getting friends.
The badass roadies take care of us.
We need their expertise.
Getting it out there
hurts nobody.
They're all waiting to hear it.

A shame of blame. A blind of bliss.
For the good reason
we don't mess meeting
with honest artists.
We don't want politician's predicament.

The ebb and flow
of the mob run amok.

Shortened hair and joined
OK, it's two people who got this,

the fame screwed in
hanging in tight
keeping us together.
Where we're going next
is a different matter.

I'll never forget us doing this.
I'm never so drunk that I can't
remember us doing a song.

Sing for you
is this girl's virtue.
Don't take it away from you.
It's not a virtue
without a star.

# Rachel Cusk

American novelist

(her voice)  —after *Kudos* (the novel's final scene)

It cut a figure in such a
compelling way, of a man
standing in the sea-waters
peeing on the leg of a woman,
a scene so repugnant yet
true, a sordid fact of life
for women in a world
where sexual violence
is a commonplace occurrence.

# Mary Gaitskill

American novelist

(her voice)

The wherewithal of a woman's intelligence
is not bound up with her dignity—though it
helps to have it in spades. It is, rather, bound
up with her self-respect, which, when it
comes at you full-throated and climactic,
threatens to blow you away, or at least
undo your previous assumptions. And she,
for her part, feeds off this prospect as only
a fixated lover can, ignited by the lust
for control, or the loss of it, which she inspires,
that will take you to new places, to places
you never knew existed before. This kind of
intelligence is neither feminine nor masculine,
it transcends gender. Yet such a woman knows,
too, that her sex is the root of all desire, male
or female, and that baring it in the use of her
intelligence reorders the psychic structures
by which sex most fully functions. So her brain-
power being sexualized and eroticized both
at the same time, gives her body what it would
otherwise lack: desirability, or possessed of
erotic charge which her electric thoughts
disseminate one word, one sentence at a time
until you, struck as if by lightning, behold her
in a wholly new light, she now master of her
fate, and, perhaps too, underminer of yours.

# Diane di Prima

American poet

i   (her voice)

I negotiate the landscape
by what I know, until
what I don't know
becomes the landscape.

How different we all are
each following our own star.
We tend toward the light
then back away, it's too bright
for us to see by,
but all the same we try.

The twist of irony in all our lives,
the gods say, is we must die.
But we'll be the gift you'll have
to receive when we're gone.

ii   (her voice)

A day old, or a million years old,
what's the difference? The phylogenetic
primitive human being is presently alive in us.
We connect with him or her only when
the channels are open, which for most of us
 remain blocked—out of sight, out of mind—

until a trigger unleashes a code
we've all but discarded as useless,
powerless, even voiceless. But listen again…
The voice still can be heard, a faint trace
of roots on a wavelength sleep maintains.
The waking we celebrate, however, won't
allow for the nod that once was as god-like
as imagination, and as free. It's chained now,
behind a barb wire fence where it roams
to scare off unwelcome intruders.
Thrown meat, it'll snarl, then snag
the traffic coming and going for
a while, before hungering for more.
The less it's fed, the bigger
it looms in the shadows.


iii  (her voice)


The debate on dreams—
do dreams matter? and if so, why?—
is the same debate on poetry—
does poetry matter? and if so, why?—
that continues ad nauseum in our time
and in the current culture.


A read despicable for
its contraction of
language's capacity for
surprise found in its rebirth?


dreaming is to the nocturnal imagination
as poetry is to the linguistic imagination

The powers that be that determine what gets said and published
amplify the status quo at the expense of the unseen and unheard.
But somehow the latter finds a way. They always do.

A mystery that doesn't materialize
is like untasted food.

The banal is anti-climactic because
nothing is really at stake except its own survival.

One word can conjure
a world, or a memory of one.

The brain has scrolls
of its own you can't see
the end or beginning of.

Speech is a variety of poetry
that can't be pinned down.
It moves through the air
like gold dust.

Everybody knows we built civilization
on the back of speech, but consolidated
its power by writing it down.

Please give me the vessel
that's behind all this:
      Woman.

# Charles Bukowski

American poet

(his voice)

I'm now sitting down here with my eyes open wide
having a front row seat to my nature (such as it is)
where once I was afraid
to admit the horrors of my
hatreds & hideousnesses & jealousies & envies &
murderousnesses
I'm now sitting down here with my ears glued
to the sounds of the river
of life rushing by
where once I tuned out
and flew high as a kite
in the blue firmament of the sky
I'm now sitting down here on my grave
with death holding up the stars
I can see better by
(when at night I'm lost and alone and afraid)
I'm now sitting down here wagging my tongue
—my mother's tongue?—
like it's going *in* style and in my father's land
there's a tomorrow

# David Rigsbee

American poet, critic

(his voice)

What regulates the language of poetry
is speech—how we speak to one another
in our daily rounds—not rarified or
elevated above our search for a language
we try to make ourselves home in.
Yoda-speak, therefore, enhances only
some ennobled view of language that
nobody actually uses. Use is key to poetry—
its sound and weight and resonance
in the common discourse is what makes
it both listenable and trustworthy.
Anything else is suspect. That which has
registers all over the place, is a challenge,
to be sure, to conventional notions of lyric.
The names one ends up giving to one's voices
will go a long way to keeping readers
interested, as well as invested, in
the forward flow whose motions, like
tides, are defined by the push of name
and the pull of fame. It's this game
we all want to be part of, if not win.
Identity politics aside, we all need
a name to steer our lives by, the boat, if you will,
we can make waves with being the minimum.
Sails will take one further, however, so let

the winds of fate blow any which way, and
hang on tight to the tiller if you've got places
to go. Names will get you there quicker,
is what I'm saying. Story-wise, it'll make
the mix fresher, more alive, and take wholeness
higher for being on the lowdown.
East or west, the best face forward is one you recognize
each time out, else what's the point of naming?
This only my point of view, of course.

Camera-ready lines tossed from your ship's prow
into the wavy deeps engraves the stars we see by tonight.

Meanwhile the future beckons to us all.
Stay tall and keep fighting against the fall.

# Simon Perchik

American poet  i.m. 2022

i (his voice)

You have touched the depths that
not even Father of Stones knew
were there, in a manner of speaking,
as you would say. The said, though,
as you know, is no bargain, and never
has been. What a price paid Nature
exacts, one letter at a time, don't I
know it, for all my supposed wisdoms.
Where would your sky take you next
if not to the latest view of the desert
where travellers come and go, vanishing
into the sands and the sparkling mirages,
I among them too many times to say,
the way, as Dante immortally wrote,
lost, and believe me the day did not
wait for its children to be found before
night devoured our bones. I'm here
to tell the story I want no part of.
But the true has tried me, who am guilty
of tossing the ship's manifold into
the sea of infinity, and me following suit,
washed ashore among the stones,
my home away from home, without end.

Mind you, minding
time & space is all we poets do
and even more so the older
we get. Witness myself, a
tree in the storms of life
that'll bend, not break, though
ache I do for a forest of trees
to keep me company. The
sand dunes and tall grasses
are all I have, a seashore
to walk up and down on, on
cloudy days, or sunny. A friend
in need is a friend indeed.

ii  —after a poem of his

He spares no one, least of all himself,
from that bivouacked mindset before battle,
every portion of despair at the thought
of dying mixed with its opposite—repair
of the heart still holding on, a holdout
to the blanketing snow winter pours down
from overhead, from heaven's ocean
he sees reflected in waves around him
of now short, now long odds of survival.

# Jack Spicer

American poet


(his voice)


Mysterious radio signals from deep space detected.


Spirits are all around us,
    everywhere…


*


Order by heart.


I'm ready.


Algorithm in the
key of free.


Beware of what
you can think of.


You can nip it in the bud.


Let the meandering
snake of a tale
tell itself.


A lot of people…

Not me.

*

I am the ghost writer of me…
Please give another year to me
in the green zone of wild grass.
Everyone else is a prophet but me.
You will meet a tall dark stranger who is me
and is the father of my children.
The kids are all right like me
yet I feel the inception of winter's bone in me.
For I am the ghost writer of me.

*

Channeling is not part of the modern
American skill-set, as it were.
Trance is shunned as a devolution into
the third-world mind, or worse, the primitive mind.

Ghosted language is disembodied
language, where even poets—
you'd think otherwise—spend most of their time.

I want what
language doesn't say
because language won't say
what I want.

There are so few selves
that people projecting them
show up for.

I'm too busy hiding
to be found wanting
what I already have.

Zooming in blows up the
details that god is in.

Climbed the vine to heaven
with his seeds, did Jack.

And it's a wound
climbed down from
on the side
of the sun.

Have news,
will follow.

# Charles Simic

American poet

(his voice)

The flow I'm not going with is carrying me along.

Our own traumas create the stories we live out of.

Time is a hook, we know, a crooked tale it tells.

The galaxy the gods inhabit is inside you.

Love's customized embrace—smaller than actuality,
bigger than possibility.

Clear-eyed enthusiasm beats deluded ego anytime.

The heaven that cuts the cord to hell will die.

Vulnerabilities of a persona is in defense of a person.

On the back of your mind watching the show,
memory rewinds on fast or slow.

Every outworn self is kindling
 for the next self arising out of the ashes.

When the unknown is finally known,
it will be renewed.

Constancy is the handiwork of the instant
in the guise of repetition.


What does a daisy give?
A daisy gives a fig.
The lotus, though, blossoms
from the inside out.


How would you like to get clear
 of the fog of fear? he asked.
Use, not abuse, night's inspiration.


If the early crow has the first
word, what does the dawning sun have?


Knew what I was in for when I dreamed
I was a young ass or goat, but found out
it wasn't a dream, the braying
wouldn't stop, I kid you not. The lout
I am, of course, still unredeemed.


It will be as it is,
wasn't it?


Niches he fought,
destinations he sought.


Hourly wages
of poetic pages
add up penniless for
would-be sages.

Why do we see things while dreaming
without using our eyes?

I don't know anyone who
is rich in the face of nature.

I hear Imagination say
to Reason:
I defer to you
in all matters,
 except what matters.

Holy inspiration can withstand anything
but the surrender it requires.

If all oceans could be believed I'd always
go toe to toe with every wave hugging
the shore.

# Arthur Sze

Chinese-American poet

—after some poems of his

To the milkweeds they go, the monarchs, overwintering
by the millions as far north as southern Canada, in sync
with their life cycle anchored between oyamel firs and
milkweed, from egg to caterpillar to chrysalis to butterfly,
as I walk along the road in Kita-Kamakura to the rice paddy
early in the morning, the dew in the air settling as I scan
the netting overlaid upon the stalks we saw planted in spring,
the railing I now stand in front of an October omen
of obstacles to come, part of the procession of events
unplanned for yet not unwelcome as I glance ahead
to December, its music of ice refracting on my
eyelids momentarily shut, then upon reopening
I peer across the mud-soaked paddy to the houses
turning on their lights, as I recall last night's
visit to the hill for our impromptu look in the darkness
at the star-filled sky, hoping to see a comet or two
thinking—if there is for us wisdom to be found,
how does one apply it, is the question.

# Grace Paley

American author

Like the time arguing with a friend
on a downtown Manhattan sidewalk
(Houston Street to be precise—though
west or east of Broadway I can't recall) when
fed up after our tiresome feud I
got down on my knees right there and
then and begged forgiveness for
having offended "Grace" no less (writer Grace Paley
that is, hosting a reading we had earlier attended
on the theme of 'Women and War,' and I, among
members of the audience invited to the microphone,
came to center stage and, bending low, announced
"She stoops to conquer…" to mostly silence and
stifled 'hee-hee-hees,' giving offence to my
dear friend, to whom I would afterwards kneel
on the sidewalk, supine to the cosmos, salaaming
with back bent, kneeknobs on cement)
when suddenly —by sheer grace?—a stranger jogging
past called out to me in passing "You're forgiven!" before
disappearing forever from sight (but not from mind…)
And in that moment like a rose aroused from sleep I,
in the church of my new ears and eyes, arose
and together down that sidewalk we paraded off
in smiles and laughter (my kind of happily ever after)…
until this day this poem has come in which, as a stranger
once bore me witness I now, if I can, would bear
my memory witness in the eyes, the holy eyes of Grace.

# Jim Harrison

American poet

(his voice)

I tied my fortunes to the tide
of events that, come what may,
I rode like waves to the shore,
each day a saturation of plenty
filtered through an instant's
bliss, "all of the prism's
colors, birds, animals, bodies,"
until satiated by the procession
entire, from predator to prey,
I was led to the conclusion:
Bigger than death is the voice
of truths that rings down through
the years, but bigger than truths
is the death of the voice
rung through tears.

# Robert Creeley

American poet

(his voice)   —after "The Warning"

In dying, we give
ourselves to the living,
whose heart becomes
now an urn…
May we be received
there in grace
to occupy a hallowed
place beyond ignominy,
beyond the gravity or
grandeur of redemption,
where love is
not dead in us.


*


To meet one's extinction
is just one more moment
in time, and attachment
to the body will have
faded away and dissolved
into universal consciousness.

# Joseph Stroud

American poet

(his voice)

There are those whose breaths
are not measured, whose deaths
over time amount to less
than the constituted loss
of their lives and loves, whose
memories are not part of the worldly path's
continuance, which point to larger truths,
here deferred, that coalesce
as these words far, far beneath,
by which a once lost faith
now returns as bliss,
darkly, like a kiss
through the fire's wrath
(or is it warmth?)
reminding heaven of mortal, haunted earth.

# Maxine Kumin

American poet

—after *Where I Live: New & Selected Poems*

She mines her extraordinarily ordinary
days on the farm for the poems they are
or would become, tasking her intellect
to clear the underbrush and her heart
to winterize the rooms she lives
unsentimentally in, feeling the pulse
of her days tempered by the sure
knowledge it would end, horses,
cows, dogs and birds all short-lived
reminders of the wheel of life turning
to the rhythm of the circling stars.

For she lives in the patterns she's making
from the days filled with aching
which she tries, with words, to salve.
Let the nights, she says, resolve
around them these lines I scatter
to the winds, where cosmic chatter
joins in effortless rhyme, the bitter
and the sweet—could there be any other?—
and let my heart's eyes retrieve what's
loved well enough, as a self's harvested fruits.

# Asian American Poets

(their voices)   —after *Poetry*, July/August 2017

Began like you, ended up me—
a wholesale commodity given
away for free?
                ...Reclaimed,
the anointed clay of my meager
tongue is named, and I grow
a foreground I can escape at will,
world gone under for the terrors
visited from above. Where
has spirit gone in its going too
far, by the star I hurl myself at,
the sound of our breathing night
not surrendered to but spoken for
at last—
                ...what, poetic gold?
We are in a shitty age,
we say, it's coming out of
our anuses our mouths our
eyes our ears, a shitty time for
us all to be living & dying in,
especially those of us on the run
from the powers-that-be that no
amount of metabolizing we
shit-stirring poets do, can fix. So
such being the way of the world,
we say, the rear you should
stick it up
is your own.

If the crux of the matter is
the 'curse' of matter,
a line the mind cannot cross
without accompanying dross,
may the buoyant ball
stay bouncy
through it all…

The father slain,
the mother lain,
how stay sane,
child, without blame?
Accuser time
is secure as rhyme
as judge and jury
you cannot bury.
You'd go your way
have your say,
but others misunderstand
your giving hand.
So instead
of playing dead,
you grow strong
by your song
where day is
night wedded
by the work
the dark
does.

# Lucille Clifton

American poet

(her voice)    —after an interview w/ Chard DeNiord

It doesn't matter if you
let yourself in or not.
It's time I went to do
my work, not that it
matters all that much,
but that's just how I feel.
We've walked up the stairs
of my life and told stories
that have got me here
one way or another, and for
that I'm grateful. But don't
tell me it hasn't been hard—
what the losses add up to
as a life lived, grace
leading the way or not.
Either way I'm done, a bare-
stripped heart is no tell-all.
But I hope in the darkness
that follows I'll have let in
a little bit of sun.

# Allen Ginsberg

American poet

The time poetry takes to climb
into consciousness from the underworld
defies all, or almost all, readers including poets
themselves who do the yeoman's work
to get there, into the light of day, that is,
where words are relished as spoken jewels
adorning the mind with nuance
born of pleasure as well as pain.

But I forgot all about poetry and wasted time
feeling lonesome catching the wave of memory
shoreward to New York's East Village where
I courted my future wife who birthed us a son
at nearby St. Vincent's now an upscale condo,
gone the spectral view from its window
that icy winter morning he was born,
gone the holy suspense in which we
have been kept, the passing years here
in Nippon a refuge of sorts not from
the world's evils mind you but from
personal demons getting the better
of me, the angel's blessing I'd wrestle for,
Zachriel's, whose message to me now is
you're never far from who you are be-
coming in the light, the light of love's rewind
in which, as I bend closer to hear, Ginsberg to me says:
*Widen the area of consciousness.*

# Part Nine

*Everywhere star*
*of everywhere.*

# Albert Einstein

German-born theoretical physicist

i    (his voice)   —after a letter

The language of things is thingy,
delivering impressions started who
knows where, formed who knows how,
given meaning who knows why.
Science clears the way to the answers
in a language of concepts, whence comes
consciousness, by definition, connecting
data and the mind observing or analyzing
it, brainfood by any other name. Yet I
am the child of imagination, not knowledge,
though the passion to say so adulterates
the words I use in saying so.


ii


"He was struck that planets, stars, and other celestial
objects all pull on each other."
              —Michael Dine on Albert Einstein


How we see or imagine the world
pales beside how we treat one another
in the day to day affairs which make up
what we call the grand scheme of things,
is the point Einstein makes in his last
letter before dying, a letter that sold

for millions in a recent auction and
that still speaks to us so many years
later, that I've been moved to paraphrase
and pay homage to here, resolute
in my grasp of essentials I live my life by,
or try to, though never without the thought
that if I can only word things better
in daily life, the world would need less
writing wasted on a 'cosmic religion'
of the way things actually are
that, yes, can be evidenced by gazing up
into the inexhaustible night sky.

# Martha Heyneman

American Gurdjieffian writer

—after *The Productions of Time*

i   (her voice)

Tell me the tale and I'll tell you
without fail who the hero is you
wish to be. Tell me your story
and I'll feel in its contours your
dragon draining you of your power.
But let the hour come, however,
for you to behold what you desire
in your inmost self, and give it birth
and life from the energy that, limitless,
you have tapped into— such a telling
will unfold a new ending, where Love
pushes and pulls forth the self, in
wishing to be, that already is

doing something other than what was
uniquely itself, but merging itself with
Otherness, a unity in unprecedented form,
conquest of the self giving way to a new
context, a diviner reality: you can see it
in a wheelchair, properly understood, where
the wounded healer sits and meditates on
the world at large, as good as it all is, reading
it—the truth—from ever newer points of view:

the strange fact is, she removes her clothes,
his Muse does, and thus naked, takes into herself
his hunger, of which she herself is the cause,
and both feeding on it and off it gives him
the gift of the world as she embodies it,
his deep-rooted hunger for meaning that
you, whoever you are turning this over in your
mind, would do well to consider, before proceeding...

for the Airyland he takes into himself in great gulps
of air, oxygen that these tales are via the lungs, into the heart
where circulates the blood whereby he not only
survives, he revives, and thrives—the Airyland alive to
what he can't see but which runs through the visible
world at every point and at every moment— is that
which... once upon... a time... is... ever after.

ii  (her voice)  the sun

The sun I don't dare stare at
has me beholden to it, or is it
to him or her? I cannot say,
or again, dare not, at risk of
falling towards my primitive
ancestors in terms of outlook,
which won't do in our scientific
age. Still, the sun's warmth and
all-pervasive light as energy
source for our lives is god-like,
and to not acknowledge its
presence is willful blindness
I won't indulge. The blazing sun
is not anything less than my

maker, if it can be conceived
as such, and we share this planet,
as living beings, because of its
billions-year old light streaming
down from, yes, the heavens.
The sun, then, worships us as
dust motes in its eye. Why
shouldn't I worship it for its
presence in the sky, real and holy?

# Prospero & Miranda

—after Shakespeare's *The Tempest*

i

The ideal of Platonic forms eternally
present behind the veil of appearances
has been with us for millennia, con-
tributing to the divide that, for the past
five centuries, opened between body
and soul. Such a gap, however, moment-
arily closes when, say, two people kiss.
Their liplock transcends all categories,
likewise do the stars they see in each
other's eyes. Space occupied thus, as
haptic knowledge, makes time habitable.

ii

He doesn't have any idea, Prospero
mapping the stars in his eyes, how
the head for all its hardness loses
its place along the way so easily
that no island adventure can put it
to rights again. He would burn
his book before he drowned it,
but the ashes would muddy the
waters in which he's able to swim.

# Carl Sagan

American astronomer

(his voice)

I'm on a wavelength of scientific
observation and verification, where
faith crumbles on its foundation of
the unseen. To me, the cosmos we
now can see into further than ever
before, points to our existence
floating as a mote of dust…
like the blue dot on which we live.

# Keith Frankish

British philosopher

(his voice)

The panpsychists among us have it
that mind lives in matter comprehensively,
so that down to the minutest particles
mind functions—or consciousness—that
brings an aggregate identity to life.
How on earth does everything have
consciousness that others can experience
is one question. While the other is,
we may know how a particle behaves
but how do we know its intrinsic
qualities a la consciousness? It's too
far-fetched a star to navigate the world
by, is how I see it. But seeing is a pauper's
game. The trick is in knowing. Still
and all, what we know about consciousness
is by names we build it by, a limbo
I'm comfortable in, for now. Both heaven
and hell can wait! Enchant me some
other time, poets!

# Carlo Rovelli

Italian physicist

i   (his voice)

Time—or what we understand as time—
is not on the side of our species. We will
not outlive the damage we are doing to
the planet. Ours is a mortal existence,
as a species as well. We human beings,
were we to revere nature, of which we
are a part and to which we belong as
to our home, might stand a chance
of surviving, but we have made nature
our enemy, objectified her, removed
ourselves from the natural order, at
our peril. Space and time are mysteries
that continue to exert an influence upon
our imaginations, even as we peel away
the veils. We interact with one another
across space and time in ways still
unimaginable. To be human is to be
one species among many. Even as our
chances of survival grow dim, we remain
curious about the wonders of the fathomless
cosmos, interwoven out of things both
seen and unseen, known and unknown,
imagined and beyond imagining.

ii (his voice)

I am at wit's end to call forth the muse
of science when the Earth has refused
the poet his entreaties time and again
due to centuries of unforgivable abuse,
so, I return to the ancients who contain
in their works the clues necessary for
a song of new knowledge to appear,
were we able, in our hubris, to hear
what Brecht, Musil, Milton, and Lucretius
(for starters) corroborated in terms for us
scientific and poetic supremely interwoven,
a filigreed text of data, numbers, and emotion
imagined and written at the height of devotion
to truths once hypothetical now a revolution
made palpable under the watchful eye of Venus,
heavenly goddess par excellence, luminous
in her aspect embodying the light of science
in our disembodied world, where conscience
is now a disenchanted voice sounding in the abyss.
(Or as Joyce put it, In the beginning was the woid.)

# Quantum Theorist

The text you write is a gravitational field
from which the reader is not distinct.
There are no mysterious forces birthed
at its center—it is the signs that cause
the symbols to resonate, or not, in the mind
so that the text comes alive. The reader,
however, processes the text on different
levels. On one level is the conscious
mind where reader and writer intersect,
information-wise, for all practical purposes
separate but distinct. But on another level,
the unconscious, words and their meanings
slip and slide, the borders blur, and
before you realize it you and the writer
are made of the same stuff. Further on,
the writer vanishes and all there is
is the reader. Wake up and dream, says
the text. Or rather, you're dreaming
the text, having absorbed its words
that have been transferred from one
point in the gravitational field to
a distant point, all the way to here.


*


Why doesn't somebody take a gun and bang!
...settle it? said Bruce Lee in *Enter the Dragon.*
A line not easily forgotten, let alone crossed.

# Stephen Nachmanovitch

American writer

(his voice)  —after *The Art of Is*

I've got my finger on art's pulse
by letting go the distinctions
such as true and false
and allowing the distractions
of past and future
to dissolve, to feature
the present front and center.
Here the breath of our surroundings
translated as the heartbeat, is a scaffolding
each footstep makes in the spaces between things
where the flow of call-and-response intermingles,
a current of tellings and re-tellings
not to be committed to writing
but to be pitched in singing,
the text hardly the teaching.

# Angel of Form

—after *Transcendence,* dir. Wally Pfister

He had transcended
the body for the home
he had lost, a compactor
tightening around
the surface of things
in his depths. It was
the force he was with,
momentarily, a path
chosen by him a story
ago that nothing around
him could help him remember
except for the love he felt
in its absence. By it,
the Angel he'd wrestled
to a standstill—on standby
now—pointed the way
homeward, a target
he would lock on if he could,
for the form, upcoming,
was beckoning from the reef
of formlessness he ventured
near in his dream. Or was it
the Angel commanding 'Let go…'

# Anthropocene Blues

--after *ANTHROPOCENE: Climate Change,
Contagion, Consolation* by Sudeep Sen


In a franchise of climate change writing, we find
ourselves mute, incomprehensible to ourselves
for the world we've created and have all but
made uninhabitable, increasingly, for those who
will follow us, the brand known as Anthropocene
our last entryway into the world we no longer
know, can no longer save from ourselves, yet
we persist in its loving creation via words, to
honor our place not as gods but as humans close
to the earth we've despoiled, close to the ground
we walk, that one day will give rise to what's best
in human experience, nature being our goal,
our standard, our dream, if we could only get
there, to arrive at the body we have condemned
out of hand, as per ethics of the gods we would
emulate, that mythos unravelling as we speak,
for it is in speaking that we lose the thread
and abandon our search out of the labyrinth
of silence, of the world without us, time
out of time our only hope now, to lead us
back no matter how long it takes to the spaces
in us that redeem time, historical time, the river
we cannot cross without the body we love,
the nature between two shores we call our own,
in which we would bathe, beauty by any other name,
were it only enough to bring us the bounty we
are part of, singular, humble, awash in mystery,
the world and our words in tandem, and alive,

now no more stories but the one we live and die for,
the one that nature, inexhaustible, is telling us in language
spoken for when in love, and in death, we are.

# Yuval Noah Harari

Israeli historian

(his voice)

The humans who would be gods
have already ascended the heights
to pronounce the future of the species:
it doesn't look good for humans
organic to their bones, soon to be
replaced by mechanical drones
with art and love on their minds,
algorithmically determined as music
will be. To become obsolete in the shadow
of what's coming, is our fate:
don't be late, the gods will insist,
and we, tearing up nature's contract
in the bargain, will be beholden
to those who seek to replace us—
*homo sapiens, homo deus, homo abeo.*

# Riccardo Manzotti

Italian philosopher

(his voice)

The who of our identity is through the world
surrounding us that we experience moment
to moment, not in ideas nor in neurons, but in
the objects we see, hear, smell, taste, touch,
the separation of subject and object a myth
of physical reality. My experiencing a writer
is an identity between the writer and what I am
and experience. I *am* the writer. My brain
does not 'partake of' the writer. The writer
is the writer, and my reading of the writer
is a function of the identity that is constantly
expanding, as world, as consciousness hidden
in plain sight, where you are and I am are one.

# Patrick Fugit

American actor


(his voice)  —after *Almost Famous* dir. Cameron Crowe


According to the fact-checkers, who says what
must be established, either confirmed or denied, as
those things people say when the plane's going down.
In effect: See you in the real world, I hope…
Yes, now you know. Each voice is an S.O.S.
and he who is channeling them has already
reached paradise, is already dead, in heaven &
almost famous…, the hells and purgatories
he passes through passing through him to
return him to where he is renewed in the depths
of his being (dead)… while keeping yourself alive, you
who are hearing him 'live,' are hearing yourself.

# Neil Armstrong

American astronaut

—lines inspired by a *New York Times* article

Is there a mirror on the moon?
…What Neil and Buzz left on the moon
is ringed by footprints, sitting in the moondust
of the Sea of Tranquility, put there an hour
before their final moonwalk, and years later
is the only Apollo experiment still running,
by which we can 'ping' the moon with
laser pulses to measure very precisely
the Earth-moon distance and learn
about the moon's orbit, how the moon
is spiraling away from Earth 3.8cm a year
because of the ocean tides, how it has
in all likelihood a liquid core, and how
the universal force of gravity is very stable.
Who knows what else they'll discover,
what coming new twist in the arena of space-time?

*

The moon is falling
not from, but
into, the sky above.
We watch, mesmerized,
from below.

*

Not to peel back layers
of what you can see
but to add layers to what you can't see
about yourself, and the world,
is the human task.

i.e. the moon I've never been to
is up there still out of reach,
yet made all the more real
for my imagining it.
Has mankind really been to the moon?
Not yet.

# History Dreaming

i

We have to have history hold us
in the hot sun of time lest we melt
away to the liquid streams inside us:
we have to have history honor the ground
we stand on where so many lie buried
lest the soil consume our bodies whole:
we have to have history so help us god
because without it we would let go
our identity and slide into eternity.
History, then, defies death in the end.


ii   to the brave historians

Gone down into the mire of history
to feel vicariously the trauma of the past
puts you at risk of not coming back up
into the light of the liberated present,
which is what you seek after all,
the present liberated from the unseen
horrors of human degradation and violence
that every nation's status quo resists.
Keep it locked away is the prevailing m.o.
but for the historian's willingness to
imagine the worst of our experience,
to empathize with the victims who
otherwise, would never have a voice.
The dark past revisited courts disaster at

every turn where humanity recovered
is on the line, one's own and the world's.


iii


Late in life the love I've lost is historical:
Mangar Bani, Ashur, Troy, Tulum,
Stonehenge, Pompeii, Uxmal.
Time to remember, time to hold on
to images that come and go, as I recall
the past and all its glories, of olden
tales of kings and queens and local
heroes that the times, ah yes, embolden.
For the love I've found has kept me full
of nerve to weave the ash with the golden.
I will not ask for more than this: to feel
today, while to last night be unbeholden.
Let my dream-others bring back the me
to myself, and the dream back to reality.


*


Sweetness without the badass
is cloying. History without
mystery is toying.


I subscribe to the truth.
It arrives every morning
at my doorstep, somewhere
between sleeping and waking.

iv

Did you think sleep was a dead time?

Dreams are more than wave tracks in the ocean of time and
space.

What comes forth in dreams
radiates night's heat
the heart, mind, and body
will replenish by.

O night, bountiful night
bearing all my dreams.

I know why we dream:
The oracular night has
messages for us to read, yes;
and the day's events pass
through transformed, it is true;
and the toxins of our lives are
cleansed, without a doubt.
But the real reason we dream
is so we can dream each other's
stories and enter the mystery
of otherness on its own terms,
sans logic, sans meaning, sans deadlines.
Look for rhyme and reason
and you won't find them. But look again—
poetry is dream's native language.

whether we dream at night
or we dream in the daytime,

sleep is
what dreams are made of.

Here's what sleep does: dreams of poetry ops.

Our human understanding and experience of time
was constituted from dreams.
The first poem was written in a dream.

From their dreams, human beings created time.
Our early ancestors called it dreamtime.
We moderns call it time past, present, and future,
or history when self-interested national politics entered the
picture.

Dreams work by compression. As do poems.

Dreams are the soul's hypertexts
composed of energy exchanges that generate
images sprung from the five (or more) senses of the body.

Humans taking dream imagery literally,
no doubt produced the first figures of speech.

Rhyme, assonance, alliteration
are all found originally in dreams.
Hence do they find their way
naturally into poems

If the line to god is indeed dead,
then we are merely talking to ourselves.

The soundtrack to your life, where
the music fits, is your dreams.

I overhear the world in my dreams.

All dreams are originating. That is why
we dream: to return to the source.

Dreams offer new airwaves for channeling real life.

I do not say,
I had a dream.
I say, I have a dream
which nobody can put a bullet through.

Dreams reprise the day's lies, undisguised.

Dreams projected on
the screen of sleep
is life re-lived, poetically
charged by Eros.

Time kissed his weather-beaten lips.

Time is the first and last mirror
in which we see ourselves.
Everything in between is space.

*

I never knew where the moment was
until one day night rose
in my mind's eye clear and cold
as ice. The burning I felt
in the sun I saw, made me new.
I knew then I make the sun
rise not with prayer but with rhyme

so the ten thousand stories were one.
I wanted to be grounded in history,
after all, before history ground me up.

Just remember this—
all seeing
is loss on loss
in time's fray.

In the space
of a time remembered
the face will change
and the heart rearrange.

The estranged self redeemed
by the fabricated self is a trope
of our modernity that has legs.
We can go places with it.

It's not all relative, it's just that different
rules apply as the situation changes.

If identity is fluid and contextual, then who are we?

…Time off the hook?

It bends, the self does, and breaks
open for the new self being born
right under the stars where you are,
says the poet to his pulsating avatar,
and together they walk off into the night.

# William Heyen

American poet, critic

(his voice)

Alan the cojones you've got I won't deny
but the whirling dervish you conjure misfires
in my book, since I decide which direction
it comes and goes, not you nor anyone else.
I have performed the poetic self for all
to see, and that's good enough for me.
You, on the other hand, have hidden it away
in some faraway version of selflessness
I want nothing to do with, a plot to unravel
history's cathedral I've helped build up and will rest in
when my time comes. You see, that's what
time is for, to my eyes and ears, that the years
have confirmed, pains and losses notwithstanding,
the victory over the body that I claim
as man's, the male principle, the masculine
cherished beyond all flesh, the goaded son
in perpetuity, my target ultimate as the sun.
Yes, now you know how the moon was won!
For her crown of stars, I alone am the one!

# Leonard Bernstein

American composer, conductor

(his voice)  —after *The Unanswered Question*

The wars we've visited upon our species
have upended our notions of ourselves
beyond the mass destruction of the century's
legacy we call the twentieth, our Faustus
found in our music bargaining with more
than death, with Time itself to restore
each note, each momentary pulse of life
we cannot but feel is ours and ours alone
to live, without guilt or a need to atone,
as individuals in the face of unending strife.

# Lewis Hyde

Amercian cultural critic

(his voice)  —after *Getting Past the Past*

Hoist the flag of self and identity
for all to see, and let community
be formed and solidify around it,
to give it legs over the course of
time, for events to accrue as history
and buttress the notion, in the space
of trauma and slaughter, of nation,
or its essence, power ad infinitum,
with certain inconvenient narratives
consigned to oblivion, until, that is,
an art for loosening the hand of
collective thought is learned and,
for the future's sake, put into practice.

# Mario Livio

Israeli astrophysicist

—after *Why*      (his voice)

Why not learn why we want
to know the unknown. Perhaps
we will stumble into a place
we can call, for a time, home,
that grace to which belonging
comes naturally, by which
the world's marvels resonate
deep within, replenishing us.
Why not call the need for inquiry
the human need, that stirs our
creativity and our minds to
love what we can never know.
When we do, we'll know why.

# Circles of Night, or The Last Lover

In love, I was in an ocean
between shores I couldn't see.
The ship constructed for the journey
rocked with waves of desire
that roiled within and without
knowing the way, I sailed on,
the routes of incomprehension
my guiding lines of sight.
Hold me, I said to the night,
wondering from which edge
I would fall, the moon shining
on us all, you, me, and the world
we made, one note at a time.
Sing me, I said to the sun,
and we roared like the fire
you dared me to walk through,
and, turning to the ground,
the footsteps I heard were sounds
like none other, to follow
endlessly, until I found
the kiss of life you offered,
no more pages to write of
what held me back but going forth
into this embrace, this language
close, starlit, animal, loved.

# Coda

**Morning**

i

Was it real? – or
did I dream it?
Or neither?

Through how many lines crossed have I lost
the will to believe myself singular, as the plural
lives lent in imagination's tent where, encamped,
I've listened, at times listing, to the heart's directive
leading me, not altogether hopelessly, to love
the other I am and the other I'm not, twinned
resolution of a vision I can call my own at last.

Who are we if not each other, everything sings.

What's inside inside is beyond
the hunger to feel it, and we know
time is short of space then,
belonging instead to
the heart not
of desire but of memory
that we peel back in a loop
that goes on forever, …now
a vision in
the glint of our eye.

ii

To me, the truth is yours,
not mine, to find
its way coursing like
a river between whose
banks the waves lift and
fall by the wind's tempo.
Speak to it, if you must,
in words that is an ocean
summer begins and ends
with, by autumn's sound.
Hear it at night, the bedroom
window opened to the backyard
creek murmuring its music,
and have at it when you
wake up and remember
the dream, so distant, so true.

iii

The garbage truck's chimes mingle
with the chirping of birds and the
guttural cries of squirrels to announce
autumn's morning in advance of
the fade-out shot that winter films,
with each take in between a chance
to get it right, the day's passing
into some eternal credit roll of night,
stayed in your seat for or not,
the music worth the price of admission
putting a bounce in your step as you
leave the seasons to their rounds and

look up, past the reviews, at the stars
where in your living constellation
it is skywritten—


   It's not a matter of mind over matter but
   of projecting mind into matter, that's the crux.
   After all, what the mind is made of, is what
   the universe, too, is made of. The perceiving
   subject's experience, its intrinsic presence,
   is how you or I relate to the world as wave
   function characterizes it, including particles
   that define the object of the perceiver's view.
   The materialist will have to swim to shore,
   which he may never arrive at, a ground
   as solid as it gets... welcome to 'japan.'


*** 

# Acknowledgements

Gratitude to the editors of the following publications, where some of these poems originally appeared:

*The Ekphrasis Review* (U.S.)
*NOON: journal of the short poem* (Japan)
*DIOGEN: pro culture magazine* (Europe)

**On *mamaist: learning a new language* (2002):**

*mamaist: learning a new language* may be one of the first books of poems to transpire from our global civilization. ...a joyful romp in language that is constructive rather than destructive, nurturing rather than negative. ...[It] will astonish anyone whose mind is alert to the spiritual dimensions of the language of Being, whether that person's connection to it is Buddhist, Hindu or the mystical expressions of Christian, Judaic or Islamic traditions....a major achievement.... This first book is... an important beginning for an important writer. The distinctive quality of voice and the content of his work possesses a moral tone that revels in the birth of words and meaning. This is a most exciting book, humorous, revealing, and profoundly serious.

**—Kyoto Journal**

...a wizard with language...Botsford runs rings around most poets of his generation...Like the Dadaists his title borrows and departs from, [he] throws out convention to create a new art.... not just clever language, it's a revitaliztion of old forms... he breathes new life into words by the sheer brilliance of his constructions.

**—The Japan Times**

**On *A Book of Shadows* (2003, with William I. Elliott):**

[*A Book of Shadows* is]...a wholly new way of intermingling poems by two poets, beckoning [us] to read them every which way, with mind and heart, in light and shadow, mamaist and papaist, abstract and concrete, on and on.

**—Morgan Gibson**

"A Book of Shadows" is...extraordinary in that the whole book is focused on shadows and what shadows mean. A kaleidoscope of meanings, half meanings, latent meanings! ...Mr. Botsford's narratives are flawless, carrying this reader—me—along the lines, which are an interplay of the positive and the negative philosophy, and finally makes me think this poet shares something with Lao Tzu, if I'm not mistaken.

**—Shozo Tokunaga**

### On *Walt Whitman of Cosmic Folklore* (2010):

About Walt Whitman, our most observed poet, it is easy to speak passionately but hard to speak clearly and originally. Alan Botsford does all three in the marvelous adventure of mystic assimilation that is this book.

**—Vijay Seshadri**

This boundary-crossing work of scholarship and poetic accomplishment offers a deeply felt homage to our original American Bard, a lyrical meditation on the transformative power of the poet's touch and a poetic dalliance with his twenty-first century genius. Not unlike Emerson's own figure for *Leaves of Grass* as a blend of the *Bhagavad-Gita* and the *New York Herald*, Alan Botsford's inspired performance merges the cosmic with the folkloric in an exuberant celebration of the transforming alchemy of Whitman's poetry.

**—Michael Sowder**

In WALT WHITMAN OF COSMIC FOLKLORE, Alan Botsford tackles the question: Where does poetry come from and what is it worth? His answer takes the form of allusive meditations upon, and poetic responses to, Walt Whitman's work. Throughout, Botsford seeks to reorient us toward what he calls Whitman's "United States of the Soul"—and away from the present day's "rampant consumerism, unbridled corporate greed... over-consumption, debased human values, and global ecological devastation." In some remarkable, Whitman-inspired lines of his own—particularly those of the poem "The Doorway"—Botsford does the tradition Whitman started proud.

**—Michael Collins**

Alan Botsford's book doesn't need a blurb but a broadside to be distributed in all the starstreams of the cosmic poet…If we'll read this book as it was written, with Emerson's "flower of the mind," it will enlarge our lives.

**—William Heyen**

In *Walt Whitman of Cosmic Folklore*, Alan Botsford has given us something profound and necessary: a finely and perceptively wrought affirmation of poetry's mysterious, primal, timeless, and transformative powers. Himself a poet, Botsford reconsiders our 21st century existence through Whitman's poetic consciousness—one that thought poetry to be the direct issue of the body, the soul, the very earth and stars. In an age of pervasive cynicism, the deification of technology, disconnection from our bodies and the natural world, the overvaluing of intellect and reason, and the politicization of art and literature in the academy, Botsford's book is a crucial reminder that the best poetry puts us back in touch with "the spiritual ethos of Eros" and "a living connection to the gods," without which we are not fully human.

**—Mari L'Esperance**

… a fresh, titillating look at Whitman.  …Whitman's gift to us is that he holds before us a mirror of ourselves; he shows us our potential. Botsford's book insightfully captures this mirroring effect, as I hear in his own beautiful prose and poetry echoes of the great Dionysian Bard himself.  He pays the greatest homage to Whitman by speaking back to him in fresh language but in his own voice, using his own rhapsodic tone… I think it is a valuable contribution to readings of Whitman. In some ways only another poet could do Whitman justice.

**—D.J. Moores**

Alan Botsford brings Whitman into the modern world and gives his work a whole new context in which to be appreciated, delving into need for poetry as well as the nature of making poems. Botsford's scope is wide as he imagines Whitman relative to Lazarus, Buddha, Odysseus. His work is imbued with the wisdom of the well-read.

**–Sally Bliumis-Dunn**

Deeply felt and widely knowledgeable, *Walt Whitman of Cosmic Folklore* explores the manifold ways in which Whitman's work may speak to us even in the high-tech twenty-first century.  In this spirited compilation of essays, meditations, and poems, Alan Botsford offers much wisdom about the creative process, and about Whitman's power, as Botsford writes, "to get through to us and touch us, move us, connect us to the world at our own depths where everything is not subject to use and exploitation but where each separate thing is just what it is, treasures to be found right there on the surface of things. . . ."

**—Ann Fisher-Wirth**

You have found a worthy anvil to strike your mind and heart upon... I think Walt himself would be quite amazed. He is for you I think like Rilke's ever more powerful angels--infinitely challenging for further inquiry and contemplation.

**—Jane Hirshfield**

**On *mamaist: a different sort of light* (2019):**

"After all, doesn't milk sound like a miracle?" Not dada, then, but something more nourishing, nudging the unfurl of a seed, "fern-like, out from under / every moment, a tongue, a feather, a flame lifting into the air," a smell like fresh-baked bread and rich, tilled soil….While there's mention here of the notorious nobodaddies—" Uncle-Sam-I-Am" up in the sky—of patriarchal pasts and presents, the gift of this collection is to focus us elsewhere than the phallocentric "I." Indeed, here, that "I" is surrendered to the wind of words, "a mamaist Daedalus" falling, equipped "with traits of artist and .. .rawness of answers" who nonetheless is confronted in due course with "the coming of gnomic as the cosmic of comics."

**—Spencer Dew** in *decomP magazine*

[Botsford writes] in a variety of styles and leaving us with poems that remain in memory. He calls some of his mamaist work "generic poems," by which he means poems that use "generic" langauge—everyday words and phrases—and twists them in a way that refreshes them. It's the creativity and wit in some of these poems that, I think, will stay with me the longest. … one …[is] reminded of what a poem can be by language play as lively as Botsford's.

**—David Cozy**

### On *Possessions: Poems in American Poetry* (2022):

This book boldly sets out to capture the voices and spirits of many of the most fascinating figures in contemporary English and Japanese poetry. Forging these kinds of connections over time and space provides sustenance for the soul, and as readers, we follow Botsford across the divides of time and space, identifying across eras, ethnicity, and nationality.

**—Jeffrey Angles**

I was deeply moved… an ambitious and original work…There is so much to absorb, to ruminate on and to entertain the questions the work raises…The language and imagery are often arresting—("music made for angels"—and on and on.) [Botsford's] understanding of the poets of affliction here, Lowell, for example, resonates deeply. I am touched by the heart of these poems and by the "white heat" of them. I could get lost in the connections, interconnections of it, part of the power of this work.…this work requires much time given its depth and expansivencss and what it so powerfully engenders in the reader.

**—Adele Ne Jame**

…the idea of writing a sort of epic love letter in verse to American poetry and poets is a great one. Many of the individual poems are really strong engagements with individual poets. Ones that stood out for me …. are the ones to James Tate (a perfect lyric), Anis Shivani, Yusef

Komunyakaa, Herman Melville, Mark Strand, Harold Bloom, Marie Howe, Joseph Brodsky, C.K. Williams, Jorie Graham, Louise Gluck and Charles Bernstein.

**—Michael S. Collins**

…a lovely, spirited, engaging, and erudite read…unique in its design, though clearly informed with / by/ in the tradition(s) of American and British poetry…I feel the language moves / alive on the page and it informs, and all of this so seemingly effortlessly…A most ambitious work. Epic and generous.

**—Gregory Dunne**

It is certainly a very impressive book in so many ways…the scope of the book is majestic …it's obvious that [Botsford] has a real mastery of the literature and is able to expand on it. …With "possessions" I think he gets credit for creating an entirely new genre! …the poetry holds up entirely on its own without the reader really needing to know anything about the poets themselves. Knowing more definitely helps, of course, but isn't absolutely necessary. In addition, I'm sure that the book will introduce readers to many poets they might not become acquainted with otherwise. …All in all, I found the book to be both enjoyable and impressive! It deserves a wide audience.

**—Richard Evanoff**

Prodigious…Even as his dedicated responses are about the poets, a reader is listening to Botsford revealing himself & constantly asking himself what will suffice, what can I praise & take to heart, what can I level with. I don't know how he did all this. And he, alone, could span cultures the way he does. His book astounds me for its all-encompassing energy. … I sense his book as a cosmos…. The scale of his endeavor here impresses & amazes me. All the poets who see it, who are part of his ruminations & entrances into their voices/visions will say of course more, more, but will be grateful. As I am.

**—William Heyen**

Alan Botsford has written an epic love song to American poetry, a song that maps a topography of the spirit, inspired by the works of poets from Whitman to Rankine. Through a persistent encounter with poems written by others, Botsford has found a large-enough form, an "island of remembrances, a home till the end of his now white haired days." As they have for Mr. Botsford, the 155 "duets" in this collection will also "press our human minds to hear their own singing."

**—Jennifer Wallace**

Alan Botsford's book *possessions* explores an essential aesthetic truth: namely, that the individual poet's voice takes shape over time through the deep reading of other poets. His poems, utterly his own, engage with forebears such as Walt Whitman, Emily Dickinson, and Herman Melville; modernists, ranging from Gertrude Stein to Stephen Crane, from William Carlos Williams to T.S. Eliot; and a wide array of contemporary poets. "It is in this flow I locate, such as it is, the I," he asserts in his prologue, an assertion borne out, in kaleidoscopic and startling ways, in all of the poems that follow.

**—Jennifer Barber**

After a decade-long labor of love as editor of *Poetry Kanto*—generously introducing countless American poets to Japanese audiences—Alan Botsford, now, in *possessions*, returns home to celebrate and pay homage to nearly two hundred American poets in all their wild diversity, clamor of voices, homing and homelessness, yawps, love letters, rebellions, and recriminations. It's a great homage to all of our American poets. A testament of American poetry since Whitman. Great, capacious poems. I know of no other book like this. *possessions* calls American poets to a festival, a jubilee, where each one stands in Botsford's verse like a leaf of grass in Whitman's poetic vision of democracy, brotherhood, sisterhood, and love.

**—Michael Sowder**

This book is, I think, very addictive, a page-turner, hard to put down once you start. You want to keep finding out what the poem has to say about each poet, sometimes in his or her own voice.

**—Miho Nonaka**

[Botsford's] poetry is smart and sophisticated. He has a superb way in writing in a truly original voice. This book seems destined to become a must-have for poetry lovers, and/or on any list for poetry students to read.

**—LB Sedlacek,** in *Pegasus Literary*